BLACK AND BLUE

Veronica Gorrie is a Gunai/Kurnai woman who
lives and writes in Victoria, Australia. *Black and
Blue*, a memoir of her childhood and the decade
she spent in the police force, is her first book.

BLACK AND BLUE

A MEMOIR OF RACISM AND RESILIENCE

VERONICA GORRIE

SCRIBE

Melbourne • London

Scribe Publications
18–20 Edward St, Brunswick, Victoria 3056, Australia
3754 Pleasant Ave, Suite 100, Minneapolis, Minnesota 55409, USA

Published by Scribe 2021

The words meaning 'policeman' on the cover come from various
Aboriginal languages, and were either supplied by the author or
sourced from the following article: 'Cockatoos, Chaining-Horsemen,
and Mud-Eaters: Terms for "Policeman" in Australian Aboriginal
Languages', by William McGregor, published in
Anthropos, 95(1), 3-22.

Typeset in Caslon by the publisher

Printed and bound in the UK by CPI Group (UK) Ltd, Croydon
CR0 4YY

Scribe is committed to the sustainable use of natural resources and
the use of paper products made responsibly from those resources.

978 1 950354 75 7 (US edition)
978 1 925849 24 0 (Australian edition)
978 1 925938 81 4 (ebook)

Catalogue records for this book are available from the National
Library of Australia.

scribepublications.com
scribepublications.com.au

For Nayuka, Paul, and Likarri

FOREWORD

Veronica Gorrie's *Black and Blue* speaks to the significance of remembering as foundational to Indigenous resistance and survival. Most people look to the past as a remembering of good times, of those moments we are most proud. But Gorrie's remembering is about exploring the past in all of its ugliness, with love, care, and compassion. It is this compassion that demonstrates the difference between the Black Witness and White Witness, of which Darumbal and South Sea Islander journalist and scholar Amy McQuire (2019) so famously wrote:

> While the White Witness thrives on accounts of the brutalisation of black bodies, most commonly of black women and children, the Black Witness pushes these same black women to the forefront … While the White Witness uses the language of war to disconnect us from our past, the Black Witness uses it to connect our past to the present.

In speaking of trauma, Gorrie, as the Black Witness, speaks of her own — she does not extract others' stories to centre herself as the lead character or heroine. She affords a generosity to those she speaks of, even those who brutalise her, and unlike the White Witness, she refuses to pathologise them. This is a potent example of the strength of Blackfullas and specifically of the power of the Black female writer. It is a modelling of a humanity that is too frequently denied us. Gorrie speaks of failure, of her own failure, as a mother, as a cop, and as a human being, in such a way that you can't help be reminded of what a beautiful, loving, and compassionate woman she is — a woman that we get to know throughout the book, even as a small child trying to make sense of the violence she witnesses outside her bedroom window.

This is a story of Black trauma, no question about it, but it is also a *making sense of* through the telling. And in almost every encounter, there is a reminder of Black humanity — whether the protection by a sister, the tears of a father, or the curiosity of a child. Interestingly, Gorrie doesn't delve into rich descriptions — of scent or the texture of things — so much. She doesn't want to take the reader to that place, or linger too long, because she knows too well how hard it is to revisit. She tells us what we need to know. And in doing so, we are taken into her world through the frequency and consistency of events. It is a kind of storytelling I'm most familiar with as a Blackfulla: one of events that the listener, the reader, must make sense of on their own. Gorrie doesn't pause to hold the hand of the reader, except through some humorous asides in those moments — she has a story to tell, after all. And there reads a sense of urgency in getting it out. The speed and frequency of the trauma she recounts can be hard for the reader to bear, no matter how familiar they may be with it.

As I finished the book, I was left wondering how one Black body can carry it all (knowing that this story didn't get to the *all* of it, even) and, too, I was left angered as to why so many Black bodies must carry so much of it. Yet from this comes the power and pride of Blackfullas when we assert 'still here', because our bodies know all too well the challenge of that assertion on the daily for so many of us. To be *here* in spite of it all is an exercising of our sovereignty in the most profound way possible in a settler colonial state. When Gorrie tells of the violence she experienced as a Black member of the Queensland Police Service who was advised to leave as a means of survival, she models a remembering that is foundational to an embodied Black sovereignty. She states, 'I didn't quit, though — I put the Aboriginal flag on my desk.' This is the sovereignty in refusal that Mohawk scholar Audra Simpson wrote of: not a refusal to participate, but a refusal to leave the places they deem us incapable of occupying. It is in Gorrie's remembering of her grandparents that we get a sense of the origins of this. In describing them, she says, 'The problem was, they refused to conform to town life and now, looking back, I think that's what I loved about them most.' Indeed, the daily exercising of sovereignty has always been seen, by the settlers, as a problem in this place: a problem to be solved via erasure from the landscape and from the category of human.

As the wife of a Black police officer who also retired on medical grounds, it was strange to me to recognise that with all the trauma that Blackfullas have endured intergenerationally, it is the white institution that eventually breaks our backs, or our families. In all of the talk of Black dysfunction, there is typically little space to interrogate how white workplaces end up being most dispossessing to the sovereign Black spirit, bringing the most violence into Black homes. But I think perhaps it is in our refusal to accept their account of us — daily, on the job — that the Black body is subject to the most brutality. And that is because it occurs in a place which one presumes to have been granted entry: that one has run fast enough, fired accurately enough, passed the requisite exams, and been deemed psychologically sound. There is a presumption in having met the standard for entry into the service that one has also been granted entry into the category of human. It is the constant disappointment and betrayal that we haven't and never will — no matter how much we put our bodies on the frontline for them — that is brutalising every day to the souls of Blackfullas. And this is the thing with *Black and Blue*: the most telling accounts of violence upon Blackfullas are not to be found among the interactions of the most marginalised — the Black — but in their encounters with one of the most powerful institutions — the Blue. And, in Gorrie's case, as one of that institution's members.

For some people, forgetting is integral to their survival; a forgetting that supposedly enables a letting go. But remembering what bodies must bear, must hold, reminds us of the importance of stories, and the significance of them being told. Gorrie, always conscious of how she was read — as a child, as a mum, as a cop — not only finds the power to tell her story but also claims the power of that storytelling by constantly reimagining and contesting the supposed account of her. It is glorious and hilarious. Her observations in those moments remind the reader that she is not a victim, agentless and passive. She is here to tell the truth of the Queensland Police Service, of the good and the bad. She so powerfully captures the hopelessness she felt when, having met the markers of success within the police force, she was discarded when her body could no longer withstand it.

This book could be read as a book of unbridled trauma, which could be used politically in all kinds of ways, but this book isn't for the anonymous reader coming to understand 'the Aboriginal experience'. It's for Gorrie, her children, and their children, so that they may make sense of their world — not through her as an ancestor, but right now, in their being. For the rest of us, we are reminded what it is to be human, and of the superhuman Blackfullas that enable us to be, here, still.

This is the power of the Black mother, and the sovereign storyteller. Her words, no matter how hard to come out, are a gift.

Dr Chelsea Watego

Dr Chelsea Watego is a Munanjahli and South Sea Islander woman and Associate Professor at the University of Queensland. She has extensive experience working in public health, in seeking to understand the role of race in the production of racialised health inequalities, with a particular focus on racial violence and health justice.

REFERENCES

McQuire, A. (2019) Black and White Witness. *Meanjin*, Winter 2019.

Simpson, A. (2014) *Mohawk Interruptus: Political Life Across the Borders of Settler States*, Durham: Duke University Press.

AUTHOR'S NOTE

I am a proud descendant of the Krauatungalung clan of the Gunai/Kurnai tribe, and when I speak of 'the mission', I refer to Lake Tyers Aboriginal Trust, Bung Yarnda — my place of healing.

In 2001, I began my training to become a police officer, and by the end of my ten-year career I had been diagnosed with post-traumatic stress disorder (PTSD), anxiety, and depression. Due to my PTSD, I have lost many of my memories, and I can only remember clearly the bad parts of my life.

In 2011, I started writing down some memories and before too long, I had a book's worth of them.

It is important to mention here that some of the themes and events in this memoir are not uncommon for Aboriginal people, and many of our lived experiences may be shared. My story is simply one voice of many, though; I do not claim to speak for all Aboriginal people through my recounting of experiences.

I have used words in my traditional language where possible. Although these are not defined in the text, there is a glossary at the back of the book.

Please be aware that this book contains material that readers may find confronting and disturbing, and that could cause sadness or distress, or trigger traumatic memories, especially for Aboriginal people, and those who have survived past abuse, violence, or childhood trauma.

PART ONE

BLACK

CHAPTER 1

I grew up in a small Victorian country town with my mother, Heather, my father, John, and my siblings. Two brothers and a sister. This town, Morwell, was — and still is — the coal-mine capital of Australia. It is surrounded by power stations that emit pollution 24 hours a day. Set in a rural area, and with a quickly expanding population, it used to sit on the main highway to the state's capital. Nowadays, the main highway bypasses Morwell, along with my memories.

I am an extremely proud Aboriginal woman, belonging to the oldest living culture: a culture that has survived invasion, colonisation, genocide, and epidemics of smallpox and tuberculosis, which ravaged communities and killed many. My people have survived oppression and dispossession, and yet we are still here.

I come from a long line of strong women. I don't remember much about my early childhood — and the parts I do remember I wish I didn't — but I have always known that I am an Aboriginal. We were a poor family and lived from pay cheque to pay cheque. My dad always had good vehicles, though, which he saved for. The old Holdens; they don't make them like they used to. In those days, for an Aboriginal man to own a vehicle and to have a driver's licence — man, you were something. Back in the 1970s, most vehicles weren't fitted with seatbelts, and therefore it wasn't compulsory to wear them. So, the family drive was a tight squeeze, with four in the back seat.

We had the cleanest house, and the nicest yard with roses growing in the front and immaculate lawns. My mum was so clean; she swept the floor every day and would place a page from an old newspaper on the floor, wet the end so that it wouldn't move, and use it as a dustpan. Then she would mop the floors with Pine O Cleen and place squares of newspaper randomly around the wet floor like stepping stones, so that nobody would step on her clean floor. That was the worst offence in our household and the most disrespectful: to walk on our mother's mopped floor. She was so pedantic when it came to cleanliness that I recall when she was bathing me, even from an early age, she would be scrubbing my elbows so hard she would take skin off. Apparently, she was rubbing the dark patch on my elbow because she thought it was dirty. It wasn't; what she had failed to realise is that black children have darker elbows.

What I also remember is alcohol and violence.

We lived next to another Aboriginal family: an older lady, maybe in her fifties, and about five or six children. All the children but one were over 20 years old, and the youngest was my age. Actually, I don't think the 'older' lady *was* that old, but she drank alcohol every day, and that made her look a lot older than she was. I don't think we were related to them, but I knew that they came from the same mission that we were from.

They had moved off the mission to Morwell because one of her children had been murdered. She must have suffered, because every time I saw her, she was drunk. The children were all drinking alcohol with her as well. Every night, I would hear loud arguments and fighting coming from next door. Beer bottles smashing, and the sound of furniture and other things being thrown around. The sounds were deafening and very frightening. Then screaming, footsteps, and banging on our front door to call the police. We never opened the door, but police were called. Many times, us kids would run to our kitchen window, where we had a bird's-eye view into one of their bedroom windows. The window had no curtains, so you could see right into their house.

On several occasions, I saw angry grownups smashing beer bottles over each other's heads when they were fighting. I sometimes thought that the people who'd had beer bottles smashed over their heads were dead, because they lay on the ground motionless for the longest time, but in the following days, I would see them again, and I always wondered how they survived. Cuts and blood spilling from their wounds. Often falling to the ground. Several times, while peeping through the kitchen window, I saw the youngest girl, the same age as me, sniffing something from a plastic bag. I found out later — after she collapsed, and my mum had to call the ambulance — that she had been sniffing glue. I also saw the older lady drinking white vinegar, and methylated spirits straight from the bottle. As young as I was, this saddened me.

These were the first experiences I had with violence. Though it wasn't directed at me, I still felt frightened when I heard the fighting. I also understood, at a very early age, that people who had suffered trauma and grief almost always displayed self-destructive behaviours. It was their way of coping with the extreme sadness they were feeling.

My father — a proud Aboriginal man — has always provided for his family. He always worked, had good jobs, always was and still is a good father. I remember that he built us a tree house in the backyard. The tree house was high above the roof of our house, in a large tree, and you could see the yards of our neighbours. A ladder stood against the tree to reach the floor of the tree house. It was one of my favourite spots.

I played netball as a child and can recall my parents coming to watch my sister and me play. My father would shame me out by screaming top note. I think he thought that if he screamed at us, we would play better.

Music and sport were big parts of my childhood. I come from a very musical and athletic family. My brothers played guitar, drums, and any other instrument you put in front of them. My grandmother was also musically talented and played piano. I dabbled with the guitar and sang. A lot of our family get-togethers were spent playing guitar and singing. I sang a lot with my older brother, and even wrote songs, which we recorded in the bathroom so that we could get that recording-studio effect. They were fun times, and are good memories. For birthdays and Christmas, I was the child that was given musical items. One year I got a pink stereo, the following year I got a little red piano accordion. Which I might add, I never got to master. But I had fun with it anyway. I also thrived playing my school recorder, but I think I drove my family crazy because the only tune I could play was 'God Save the Queen', which was the old Australian anthem before it changed to 'Advance Australia Fair'.

My mother was a first-generation white Australian. I don't have many memories of her from my childhood, and the ones I *do* have are not fond. The main one that stands out is of her being drunk, screaming, physically attacking and assaulting my father.

I remember a time when our family were visiting an aunt's house, which was in a tiny country town, Sale, some 200 kilometres from our house. Sale now has a Royal Australian Air Force (RAAF) base in it. It may have been there back then, but I never knew of it. We would visit often, and when we'd get there, the house would be full of relatives — aunties and uncles and cousins. The night would be a mixture of alcohol and playing cards. This would go on for hours and hours, until my parents were ready to go home, but by that time, they would both be drunk. I used to beg to stay the night because I was frightened to get into the car, but my pleas were ignored. So off we'd go; I would have been five or six at the time, sitting all cramped up in the back seat with my brothers and sister, feeling petrified because our mum and dad were arguing, which they always did when alcohol was involved. They never just argued and made up; there were almost always punches flying, swearing, and violence. I recall on one particular trip, my mum and dad were violently arguing when, all of a sudden, my mother opened the front passenger door and threatened to throw herself out of the moving vehicle. She kept the door wide open for what seemed like an eternity. At the time the car was travelling at least 100 kilometres an hour on the highway. I was terrified and didn't want to witness my mother throwing herself out of a moving vehicle, so I sat on the floor behind the driver's seat and covered my head with a blanket. She never threw herself out, but it was the longest trip home. She ended up falling asleep. I'm pretty sure my brothers and sister were traumatised by this event. I know I was! In fact, every time

I saw or smelt alcohol, whether it was my mum and dad drinking or someone else, I associated it with violence. My mother was the violent one. My dad left when I was around seven, and I was glad when he did, because I thought it meant no more fighting. How wrong I was.

I may speak badly of my mother throughout this book, but I love her with every bone in my body. I have been described as a baby animal that's been wounded by its mother, but no matter what the mother does, that baby will always return to her.

Before my dad left, the only family members we were close to were my paternal grandmother and grandfather (Linda and Carl), my Aunty Dot and her younger brother (who were my father's cousins, the children of my grandfather's sister), and Kevin.

Kevin was my grandmother's cousin's son, but my grandparents had raised him since he was a baby. He was a couple of years younger than me, and had a brother, Nicky, who we would call 'blue boy', and a little sister, Patricia. These siblings came and went all through their younger years — they'd stay with my grandparents, and then go back to their mother. They were technically of the same generation as my father, and culturally, they were our Uncles and Aunty, but because they were all younger, we never called them that.

My grandfather was very close to his two sisters, Vera and Marina. When my grandparents left the mission, they gave the house they'd been living in to Marina and her husband and their two small children. Marina was only in her mid-twenties when she died suddenly, found sitting in a chair at home, lifeless. She must have known that she was ill, or even that she was dying, because the night before, she'd had a conversation with her husband, saying that if anything ever happened to her, then the children should be cared for by my grandparents.

My grandfather was out working the land for the shire council when he was approached by the foreman, who told him about the death of his sister on the mission. Hours before the news, my grandfather said that he'd seen a white kangaroo, which is rare if at all possible. But if my grandfather said it, then he must have seen it.

My grandparents headed straight off to the mission. When they arrived, they were advised of his sister's wishes. So, after the funeral, they returned to their house with their niece and nephew, who became my father's sister and brother. Their father moved in with my grandparents as well, but they were the primary carers for the children. He died when my aunty was 16 years old.

CHAPTER 2

Almost every night, the same time every night, just as my mum was dishing out dinner, six plates, my dad's family would walk in the door. I loved it; I couldn't wait until dinnertime every day, as I knew I would see my grandfather. My mum would have to get five more plates out and take food off everyone's plate to make meals for them. Money was tight, and food was in short supply.

I was always starving, even after I ate my dinner. We had chops, sausages, mince, and fish fingers. My mum was a good cook. She did her best anyway. I really don't know if she was a good cook, or if I was just so hungry, I would eat anything dished out to me. My favourite television show during these days was *Little House on the Prairie*. My sister and I would argue about which of us was the character Laura. Television got even better when black and white became colour in 1974.

One of our family outings at the time was driving from our hometown to the mission, Bung Yarnda. They would have the local band playing in the hall, and us kids would be running around all night with the other mission kids, listening to 'Go, Johnny, Go'. Mum and Dad would be drinking all night, and then we would do the long, slow journey back home, dodging potholes, kangaroos, and the police.

I had a special bond with my grandfather; he was so funny and told me heaps of stories. As soon as he walked in the door, he would head straight towards me and rub his three-day growth all over my face until I almost wet my pants laughing. We would tickle each other and play tiggy. He was a big kid at heart and my best friend. One time he told me that he used to be in a circus that travelled around Australia, and that when he'd left the circus, he'd taken an elephant with him, which followed him wherever he went. My dad said, 'Dad, if you ever saw an elephant, you would shit yourself!' We all laughed.

Grandad also told us mrarji stories, which always scared me. He told me that he was once chased by a dooligah through the Blue Mountains while driving his car, and that he'd had to drive really fast to get away from it. Aboriginal people believe in ghosts — the good ones and the bad ones, dooligahs as well. I never believed this story, because my grandfather was the slowest driver we knew. There is evidence of this, too; he was once booked by police for driving too slowly. My grandmother would always tell him to put his foot down and go faster.

My grandparents lived in the same town to be closer to my dad and his family, a far distant world from the mission. The problem was, they refused to conform to town life and now, looking back, I think that's what I loved about them most. My grandparents never assimilated. They couldn't or maybe they didn't want to. They almost never used electricity, nor did they go food shopping at the grocery stores. They had been so accustomed to lining up for rations most of their lives and being told what to do, when to do it, by the mission managers. This way of living had been so ingrained in their everyday thinking and behaviours. Imagine never being able to move freely on or off the mission, being controlled in every aspect of your life by the mission manager. Not being allowed to leave unless you had a pass that was signed off by the mission manager. That was their reality, and the reality of many Aboriginal people. They only moved off the mission because they were told to, like so many other families before them. I am proud of them for never assimilating or conforming.

I recall many times when us kids were staying at our grandparents' house, and not by choice. I say this because they had about seven or eight cats — probably a lot more that were out of sight — and three dogs, and the house reeked of cat piss and dog shit. You never took your shoes off; if you did, you would be sure to stand in it.

They had electricity but never put lights on. So, we'd all sit around in the darkness; the only light that could be seen would be the light that was emanating from the television, which stayed on all night. Oh, I lie — they *would* have the kitchen lights on for their illegal gambling nights. Playing poker for money. This was usually on pension days, when all the blackfullas had money. They would turn up in unison just before dark; on with the light and off they would go, playing poker all night. They would start off with two-bob bets, and then the notes would come out. My grandmother would get us kids to make the cups of tea, and every now and then we'd have to get on all fours under the table to look for any money that the punters may have dropped. That was the longest I ever saw their light on — or any light in the house, for that matter. They would play cards to well past daybreak the next day.

They never had food, they never opened or aired out the house. And to make matters worse, they were hoarders. The house was full of stuff: egg cartons, newspapers, old teabag boxes. You name it, they had it. It was that bad, there was no room for them to sleep in the bedrooms. There was never any toilet paper in the toilet either; my grandfather would spend most days tearing up perfect little squares from newspapers that he had hoarded over the years to make toilet paper. It was a bit rough, to say the least, but it did the job. I now have an obsession with toilet paper. I'm a scruncher, not a folder, and I have almost always used far more toilet paper than required and have blocked up every toilet I've used. Thank you, Nanny and Grandad. I bravely asked them one day why they kept all that stuff, and I was told, 'Just in case we need it.' I'd also ask why they never had any toilet paper like other people, and they would say, 'There's no toilet paper on the mission.' I would be thinking, *well, we are not on the friggin' mission now, Nanny!*

I had a lot of good times with my grandparents. Sundays were the best days. While other families were going to church, my grandparents would load us up in their vehicle to go dump-diving at the tip. I loved it — you wouldn't believe the amount of good stuff people throw away. I would be knee-deep in garbage, scavenging through piles of crap, looking for useful stuff to take home.

My grandfather was such a gentleman, quietly spoken and gentle, while my grandmother was loud, outspoken, and intimidating. Those were my impressions as a child. When I'd grown up, though, I realised that my grandfather'd had long-term dementia, and my grandmother was a strong black woman, considering what she had been through.

———

My grandmother was born and raised on the mission, Bung Yarnda, in south-east Victoria. When her mother died in 1940 of tuberculosis (TB), she and her siblings lived with their Aunty Lou. When I was a child, I knew Aunty Lou as Granny. My grandmother's father had died years earlier, in 1935. My grandmother was one of eight children. Two of her older sisters died of TB when they were 16 and 13 years old. Her older brother, Billy, married and was in the Australian Army, but he died young as well. Her mother also had one baby that died at birth, which left my grandmother and her two sisters, Teresa and Myra, and a brother, Ronald (Ronnie).

On 11 November 1941, police turned up at Granny's house and took my grandmother and her siblings. They were stolen. The police must have turned up when they least expected them, because I know that when police or welfare turned up on the mission, the children would run into the bushes and hide until they had well and truly left.

This date is significant in Australia as the day that Australians pause for a minute — on the eleventh hour of the eleventh day of the eleventh month — to mark the end of World War I, and to pay respect to the soldiers who lost their lives. I don't, though. On this day, I reflect on the day my grandmother was stolen and what she must have gone through.

They were taken hundreds of kilometres away to the city of Melbourne, to an orphanage. It was known as the Neglected Children's Depot, Royal Park, Parkville — an institution now known as the Melbourne Youth Justice Centre. At one stage, it was also known as the Turana Youth Training Centre. Years later I was told that in Woi Wurrung, ironically, 'turana' means 'rainbow'— a bright and stimulating place for Aboriginal kids.

Within days of arriving at the depot, my grandmother's older sister, Aunty Teresa, was given to an old white woman to live with. She lived in Ararat, some 200 kilometres north-west of Melbourne, a small, dusty town that was known as a goldrush town in the early nineteenth century. She was the only Aboriginal person there. Two years later, she died. She was only 14 years old. The old white woman buried her at the Ararat Cemetery with a headstone that reads 'Therssa [sic] Gorrie'. These days, I am trying to have her exhumed and repatriated back to Bung Yarnda, back on Country alongside her siblings.

In the depot, my grandmother started showing symptoms of TB, so she was sent to hospital for tests, which came back positive. They operated on her to remove a large growth from her neck.

After her recovery, my grandmother and her remaining sister, Aunty Myra, were housed with the other girls in the orphanage, while my uncle was on his own with the boys. One day, my grandmother and aunty managed to escape through a hole in the barbed-wire fence and ran as fast as they could to get away. When they turned around, my grandmother saw her young brother crying at the fence from the boys' area. They ran back to him and tried to get him out. He was standing at the wire fence with extended arms, crying, saying, 'I wanna go home.' My grandmother and Aunty Myra didn't want to leave Uncle Ronnie alone, so they returned to the hole in the barbed-wire fence and went back inside.

After being processed at the Depot, my grandmother was sent to various orphanages for girls in the southern suburbs of Melbourne, until she was moved into the houses of white families to work as a domestic — a child slave labourer. She didn't do any of these jobs for long and ran away many times;

each time she ran away, she was picked up by police and arrested for absconding, and taken back to the depot. My grandmother never shared any memories of her time in any of the institutions she was in as a young girl. I know that she was traumatised by her experiences, though, and that this trauma has been handed down from generation to generation.

Shortly after Aunty Teresa died, the old white woman returned to the Depot and asked for another black girl to replace her. The Depot gave the old white woman Aunty Myra. Aunty Myra lived with this old white woman for years. The old white woman wanted to adopt Aunty Myra, until she found out that she wouldn't get any money from the state, so she made Aunty Myra go on a pension instead. I doubt if Aunty Myra saw any of that money.

From time to time, my grandmother would go to Ararat to stay with Aunty Myra and the old white woman, but each time, the woman would write letters to the Board of Protectors complaining about my grandmother. Eventually they stopped the visits.

Thirty years later, my grandmother, grandfather, and my father travelled together to this small town and found my aunty. After tears of jubilation, they all set off together. From that day on, my grandmother and aunty were inseparable, and Aunty Myra moved into the house with my grandparents.

A couple of years after getting Aunty Myra, my grandmother set out to find her brother, Uncle Ronnie, the man I am named after. This, however, proved a bit harder than finding my aunty, but eventually she found him at Janefield Colony in Bundoora and signed him out. He'd worked as a caretaker of the Aboriginal Advancement League in the late '70s and early '80s, until he came to live in Morwell to be with his sisters. He lived in the

Lionel Rose Hostel until he died in 1992 of renal failure.

Hostels for Aboriginal families were formed by Aboriginal Hostels Limited in all major cities across Australia. They were run by managers; this particular hostel was named after the first Aboriginal boxer to win a title, Lionel Rose, who also recorded two songs, in 1970. Years later my brother and I went to be part of the audience at a live recording of *Sale of the Century*, hosted by Tony Barber. During the ad breaks, Barber interacted with the audience by asking trivia questions, with prizes going to whoever answered the question correctly. One of the questions was an audible one, where we had to listen to a song and identify it. As soon as the song started playing, my brother put his hand up and answered, '"I Thank You" by Lionel Rose.' He won a box of meat pies. In the mid-1970s, my own father had been the manager of the Lionel Rose Hostel, and we'd lived in the manager's house.

By the time my grandmother was 16 years old, she was living and working in the Abbotsford Convent. Some nights, she would sneak out to see other Koories in Fitzroy. It was here she met a gubba sailor from a naval ship.

Months later, she discovered that she was pregnant, and she hid this from the nuns at the convent until she could no more. By then, she was heavily pregnant at eight months. The convent moved her out to accommodation for expectant mothers, close to the hospital.

We never knew who Dad's biological father was, as my grandmother never spoke about it, but she told my younger brother when he lived on the mission with them that he was in the navy and had died when his ship — the HMAS *Tarakan* — caught fire due to an explosion. My brother didn't repeat this conversation he had with Nanny until years later, when he and I were doing family research, and the name of my father's biological father was finally revealed, along with a lot of other important information. During this research, though, I found out that although there *was* an explosion and eight people were killed, he had survived, and lived in Sydney until he died years later.

All this seemed irrelevant as my grandmother entered the hospital birthing suite on that day — 10 March 1950 — to give birth to her only child all alone, with no support, no family or friends.

After a long, arduous labour, she gave birth to a baby boy; a fair-skinned child with jet-black hair and stunning green eyes. As she lay cradling her newborn, studying his every feature, nursing staff entered the room and took the baby. As soon as he had entered the world, he was removed from her. Placed in an orphanage called The Haven, in Fitzroy North, separated from his birth mother who should have been nurturing him. This new mother was told she could leave the hospital and return to Abbotsford without her baby. She left childless.

My grandmother repeatedly asked to see her son, but each time she was refused; so she wrote letters to the Aboriginal Board of Protectors and to the Children's Welfare Department, asking to visit her baby, but these letters were to no avail. My grandmother was told that in order to get her son back she would need to be married.

When my grandmother was 20 years old, and still a ward of the state, she returned to the mission with this information. She returned to the place she had been forcibly removed from: her place of birth, her sacred place, Lake Tyers Mission, Bung Yarnda. Only this time, *she* was on a mission — to find a husband in order to gain custody of her child.

The Gorrie family homestead on the mission was empty. This homestead was one of the first to be built on the mission, back in the early days. It was a tired-looking white weatherboard house with a tin roof. It stood for decades under the only lamppost on the mission, on a slight hill, overlooking the waters on which Lake Tyers Aboriginal Station — the official name of the mission until it was renamed Lake Tyers Aboriginal Trust in 1971 — was situated.

My grandmother had nowhere to live, so she moved into an aunt's house. This fibro house, with its tin roof and dusty wooden floorboards, sat where they could see the dirt road that led in and out of the mission, alongside other identical homes. An old uncle of my grandmother, Uncle Muns, had set up his humpy beside the house. He never entered the house, but always remained in his humpy. This may have been his act of defiance against the white ways. A white man's building. They said that he was a red eye: someone with special powers, someone gifted, and someone who could travel at speed, faster than anybody else.

My father told me a story about how there was a funeral that the family were attending, just over the border, and they travelled by horse and buggy to get there. The family offered old red eye a ride, but he declined and said that he would get his own way there. Well, the horse and buggy set off on a strenuous journey for the family to pay their respects. It would take them three days to get to their destination; when they arrived, who should be there and had been there for at least a day? Old red eye, and he'd travelled on foot. Faster than anybody else.

It was in this house that my grandmother met a 21-year-old man who also lived on the mission. It wasn't long before a courtship began, and soon enough, they wed at the Bung Yarnda

Church on a winter's day in mid-August 1953. This man knew of her plight and her struggle to gain custody of her child, and he supported her in doing this.

My grandmother wrote many letters addressed to the Secretary of the Children's Welfare Department, asking for the return of her son. Most were discarded and went unanswered; however, one was read. That letter said:

> Dear Sir, I was married on the 17th August to Mr Carl Turner, with whom I am now residing at the Lake Tyers Aboriginal Station and hereby apply for the custody of my son born on 10th March 1950. My husband is in full agreement with this application. Yours faithfully, Linda Turner (formerly Linda Gorrie).

This letter was recommended by the then manager of Lake Tyers Aboriginal Station, but it would be twelve months later that it was considered. The secretary approved the application, and plans were made to return the baby to my grandmother; — only he wasn't a baby anymore. He was four years old. Some months earlier, the matron of the orphanage had written a letter requesting that he be moved to more suitable facilities, as he'd outgrown his current residency. This request was granted, and my father was relocated in an orphanage for toddlers an hour away. A week later, the manager's wife, Mrs Rule, was in the city when she was notified by telegraph to collect him from the orphanage. As soon as she saw him, she told the matron that it was a shame that the child was being returned to the mother and that she wanted custody of him. The order to return the child to the mother was amended, and my grandmother was placed on a probation period, with Mrs Rule monitoring and reporting on my father's wellbeing. Mrs Rule took to bathing the toddler every day, checking for bruising or anything she could report on. My grandmother must have done well, because she kept custody of her son. My father remembers Mrs Rule bathing him, too.

CHAPTER 3

My grandmother and her family continued to live with their aunt until they were given a house of their own. Food was handed out to each family every second day of the week, distributed in bags the size of five-kilogram flour sacks. Food consisted of sugar, flour, and tea leaves. Sometimes, milk arrowroot biscuits were given out, but all crushed up, which made them difficult to eat. Meat, and milk, and produce from the veggie garden were also given out, but you had to be the first in line to get the best cut of beef. Milk was in billy cans and the butter was wrapped in paper. Bread was given three times a week, usually Monday, Wednesday, and Friday. All these rations were given out by the manager and his wife. During my grandparents' early days on the mission, there were several managers; one of the later managers introduced rice on the mission.

At this time, the only people who drove cars were police and welfare: white people, basically. Everyone else walked or got on a boat to cross the waters. So, whenever my grandmother heard the revs of a car coming along the dirt road to the mission, she would scurry my father off, and he would run as fast as he could into the bushes where he would stay until called for — presumably when the welfare and police had left. He wasn't the only child that hid when cars came onto the mission; all the children would do the same. The kids that weren't fast enough would be caught and removed from their mothers, removed from the mission. These children, like my grandmother had been, were taken to the Neglected Children's Depot in Melbourne, and then placed in orphanages or with white families around the state.

The mission had what some would describe as a 'precinct area'. There was the mission hospital, which was situated in front of the manager's home. Then there were concrete structures, placed randomly, for distinct purposes. One was a dairy, one was an abattoir, one was a two-man jail cell, and one was a bathhouse. This bathhouse had four bathtubs inside, where the children of the mission would go and bathe, using the Velvet soap that was given to them to wash their bodies. All these concrete structures still stand today, except for the bathhouse.

There was a school on the mission as well. It was behind the old church, which also still stands today. My father attended this school until he moved away. Every morning when the children arrived, they were told to go bathe. The girls would go one way, and the boys would go to the waters. It didn't matter what the weather was, they had to do this every morning. My father recalls that when it was cold, the boys used to djillawah on their feet to keep warm.

Every day at the same time, boats would come by the mission, with tourists in them. The kids of the mission would all run to strip off their clothes and jump and splash around in the water. The tourists, white people, would throw money at them; the old coins would sometimes be put in plastic bags so that they could float. These coins were used for gambling by the children, often playing two-up.

Other times when white men came on the mission, the girls and women, including my grandmother, would put sand in their vaginas so that when the white men tried to rape them, it would hurt.

My grandmother was a big gambler; when the pokies first came out in New South Wales, over the border, she would travel with my grandfather to have a punt. She also liked having a bet on the horses and playing bingo. When we were staying with her, she made us go to bingo with her every night, even if we didn't want to. Sometimes I didn't mind because at half time, they gave out free cups of tea and biscuits. That was my dinner for the night. My grandmother would give us kids her old tickets and a bingo pen, so that we could play bingo, too.

In 1961, families on the mission were told that they had to leave, as the land was being sold to make way for a resort or something of that nature. Those that left were given houses in regional areas, and many were given jobs. My grandparents' family was one of many that left; they were housed in Moe, and my grandfather given a job at the shire council.

When my father was about 12 or 13 years old, my grandparents went and worked for a white family, the Sasses, on a farm in the Gurdies. The Sasse parents, Harry and Margaret, gave my grandparents a shack on the property to live in. The Sasse family had children of its own, and my father got on well with them, and was with them all the time. Dad even attended the same school, in the nearest rural township of Lang Lang. They would all catch the bus together. My father enrolled in after-school and weekend sports: Aussie Rules and tennis. Eventually, my grandparents finished working for the Sasses, and it was time for them to move on. The Sasses told them that my father could stay with them if he wanted, and that they would continue his education and take good care of him. My grandmother left that choice up to my father. He decided to stay. He stayed there for a few more years, and even when he was courting my mother, and eventually married, he would take her to the farm, and at one stage rented a house opposite, to be close to his newfound family.

The mother of the family, Margaret Sasse, came from a wealthy background. Her father, Sir Wilfrid Kent Hughes, was a politician — both state and federal — who was responsible for organising the 1956 Melbourne Olympics. They lived in an affluent part of the city, in a big house. When Dad went there, he would see flash cars pull up, with other prominent politicians inside. Margaret Sasse wrote child-development books, and started up a children's gymnasium named GymbaROO, which is now a franchise all over the country and the world.

The family eventually left the farm and moved into that big house in the city. Throughout my childhood, I recall often going there to visit them and even now, as an adult, I have visited them often and attended functions they have, but that's about the extent of it. My father is still close to the family, though. Margaret has since passed away, but the father, Harry, is still alive and is in his nineties.

My grandparents' place was also a place of refuge to us kids. Whenever Mum and Dad started arguing, if the door was closed, we would grab a glass and put it up against the door to try and hear them. I think we saw this on the 1970s sitcom *Get Smart*. I'm not sure if this method helped or not — but looking back now, I think we were trying to figure out if the argument had escalated to actual physical violence, and if we had to get away from it.

A few times, when Mum and Dad were fighting or arguing really loudly, my brothers, sister, and I would jump out of our bedroom window and run as fast as we could to our grandparents' house. We would hang onto each other's hands for safety. We ran like we were being chased. When we'd arrive at our grandparents' house, we'd knock on the front door, but no answer; so we'd knock on their bedroom window, which was at the front of the house, and call out to them. Still no answer! We'd then go to the back of the house, to where Aunty Myra was staying, and she would let us in. Her room was small, and filled with so much junk, but we all slept together, on top of clothes that she'd placed on the floor to make a mattress for us, until daylight, when we'd return home.

Aunty Myra was deaf — she wore a hearing aid — and she heard us, so to this day I don't know how our grandparents never did. I think that they didn't want to let us in because they didn't want to get involved. As a kid, I was so scared of my grandmother. She would yell at us and call me a 'little white bitch'. I noticed from an early age that she never gave us any presents for our birthdays and Christmas. What I found out later, though, was that they didn't give us anything because what Mum and Dad gave us was always from them as well. They paid for it because, like I said, we were poor. Mum and Dad couldn't afford to buy us things, so our grandparents paid for them. I wish I had known this as a child — I would have been more pleasant towards them on these days and more grateful.

I don't recall being sick as a child — except with tonsillitis — but I was told by my mother that when I was three, and running around the yard being chased by my sister, I landed smack-bang on an opened camp-pie tin, which was just lying there on the driveway. My mum thinks this was odd, as we always had clean yards. She told me later that she thought my sister planted the tin there deliberately, so that I would stand on it and hurt myself. Apparently, there was a bit of rivalry between us girls. Every Christmas, as kids, we got identical toys and clothes, just in different colours. When my sister broke her toy, she would do a shifty swap with my perfectly intact toy. On a few occasions, she was caught in the act, and was told to give me back my doll. Well, she carried on like she was asked to give me her right leg or something!

When I stomped on the camp-pie tin, I nearly severed my whole foot. I had stitches right across it. I still have nerve problems. I don't remember this, but I have seen family photos of me with a bandage. You wouldn't believe what one of my favourite foods is to this day, though — yep, camp pie.

And there was the time when I was six and I had my tonsils removed. I really liked it in hospital; deadly feeds, too. It was weird when dinnertime came, and the food was handed out, and I never had to share my plate with anyone. Odd feeling. After leaving hospital, every time I was in the car with my dad and we saw the police drive past, he would tell me to hide, as he'd never paid the hospital bill and they were looking for me. I was petrified, I would dive practically under the driver's-side seat so that they wouldn't see me. At the time, I remember thinking if the police found me, they would demand the money from my dad for my tonsils, and if we didn't have the money, which was more than likely, the police would take me back to hospital to have my tonsils put back in. I didn't want this, because I remembered all too well what it was like with my tonsils — I always had a sore throat and couldn't swallow or eat food. I didn't want my tonsils back; I didn't want to go through that again.

My grandfather, my father, and my younger brothers were the only males I trusted. From a very early age, I thought that boys and men were scary to be around — they only wanted one thing from you, and it didn't matter what age you were.

CHAPTER 4

My first bad experience with a cis male happened when some relatives were visiting our house, and we were playing hide-and-seek. I hid under a bed — I was about six years old. My uncle, who was a lot older than me, hid under the same bed as me. All of a sudden, he grabbed my hand, placed it on his penis, and began to masturbate. I was scared and frightened. I pulled my hand away really quickly and was crawling out from under the bed when he told me not to tell. Until now, I'd not told anyone. I remember the smell of his body odour. The stink you have when you haven't bathed for a long time. From that day on, I never stayed in the same room alone with him. I felt so dirty, and wanted so much to tell my dad, but thought that no one would believe me. Later in life, when I found out that this uncle was sentenced to serve time in jail for repeatedly raping his young stepdaughter, it was no surprise.

Then there was what happened when my dad was in hospital. He had broken his leg while playing his beloved Aussie Rules football. It broke in several places and required a rod to hold it together. He was told he was never to play again, which must have broken his heart, because he was a legend at the game — I have even heard rumours that he was about to be selected to play for Hawthorn Football Club. We used to go watch Dad play footy every weekend. It didn't matter where he was playing; we would all go, the whole family, including my mum's father. Big event for us all. As a young child, it felt awesome to be the daughter of the best player on the field, and I was upset when that changed.

While my dad was in hospital, we visited him every day. It was terrible seeing him lying flat on his back, with one leg held up in the air, covered in plaster. One night, while he was still in there and I was at home, I smelt the familiar scent of alcohol, and could hear the chants of Charlie Pride. I got out of bed and followed the sound to the lounge room, where I saw my mum making out with another man. The next day, when we went to see Dad at the hospital, I told him what I had seen. I don't remember what happened after that — maybe it was so bad that I've blocked it out, like so many other memories of my childhood.

What I did find out later, though, was that that very same man was a paedophile and had raped a lot of Aboriginal girls and boys. The most heart-wrenching story I heard about him was that when he'd stayed at our house — this was prior to him and Mum making out — and after Mum and Dad went to sleep, he would creep into the bedroom that I shared with my older sister. At the time we had bunk beds; she was on the top and I was on the bottom. When my sister heard him coming in to our room, she'd jump down from the top bunk and get into bed with me, pushing me right up against the wall, because this filthy animal was coming to my bed. My sister protected me and was raped many times. Oh my god, you have no idea of the guilt and hurt I feel. We only found this out later in life, but it explained a lot about my sister's suffering and trauma. My sister had a hard life, and looking back, I can see she changed a lot around this time. To her, I would like to say, thank you from the bottom of my heart and I love you so much. I have never talked to her about this, because I don't want to open old wounds. It's just too hard.

The house where we were living then was directly opposite the primary school that we were all attending. I had so many friends and have such good memories of that school. The teachers were still caning misbehaving children at this time, but I never got the cane. I loved school and enjoyed learning. My brothers and sister, on the other hand — I'm pretty sure they got the cane once a month. On one occasion, I was sitting in my classroom, seated near the window, and my little brother's teacher came in and asked me if I knew where my little brother was. I didn't, but when the teacher left the classroom, I looked out of the window, and my little eyes scanned up the tree outside, and there he was. I just laughed, but not too loud — I didn't want to give away his hiding spot. The teacher had wanted to cane him, but he'd taken off up the tree.

Then there was the time, while in class, I saw my grandmother full-on running, chasing my sister's teacher with a boondie in her hand. She couldn't catch the teacher — lucky for him. She would have wailed on him with the boondie. After school finished that day and I went home, I found out that the teacher had wanted to give my sister the cane, but she'd run home and told my grandmother. So off Nanny went. Another time, it was the start of the day and I saw my mum prancing through the schoolyard; by the looks, she was heading towards my little brother's classroom. Apparently, my little brother had taken Dad's full set of false teeth to school for show-and-tell, while my dad was sitting home in a full suit and tie, all gummy, and couldn't go to work until he got his teeth back.

By now, we've reached the time when my dad left me with my mother. I was about seven, as I said earlier. Next thing you know, we were packing up our belongings, which consisted of a bag of clothes and some photo albums, and then we drove to my mum's father's house in a very small country town, Toongabbie. Population eight. A slight exaggeration on my part — the population might have been twelve.

My maternal grandfather — Grandad Winterburn — was born in Kent, England, in 1914 to parents Sydney and Clara, and he was the oldest of four sons. The Winterburn family came over as immigrants on the SS *Berrima*. On the day of departure, *his* maternal grandfather went along to bid them farewell, and on his way home, while walking through the streets of London, he was robbed and murdered. They didn't find out until eight weeks later, when the ship arrived in Melbourne.

Grandad Winterburn still had family in England whom he visited from time to time, including his nephew Nigel, who played soccer for Arsenal. Grandad was a concreter by trade but also built things, including a house in Drouin just before Mum was born in 1948. I was so proud of him. He married my grandmother, Hannah Brown, who was English and French, and they had four children together.

He lived on his own in this remote town, which I think he liked — every time we would visit, it seemed like he was always rushing us off. My grandfather had brought his kids up on his own, because my grandmother had a nervous breakdown after the death of one of her daughters, the twin sister of my mum. During those times, they didn't know what was wrong with her, and they gave her electric shock therapy until she was pretty much in a vegetative state in hospital. This is where she remained for the next 30 years, until she died. So, my mum grew up without a mother.

There was a local school, but it was so small that we were all in the one class. We were living in my grandfather's caravan in his backyard. This caravan had a double bed at one end, and a dining table at the other end, which folded down to a bed. So we all slept in the double bed. Talk about a tight squeeze. One moved, and we all had to move. There was no toilet in the caravan; the toilet was outside, with no lights and infested with spiders, so I held onto my pee until daylight. But even in broad daylight, I needed a torch for that toilet. The property was on acreage, with an abundance of fruit trees in the backyard. One tree I saw a lot of were the apples. My grandfather would make us white custard with stewed apples every night. I absolutely loved this meal, but my mum hated it. She told me that it was an Englishman pauper's meal, and that she'd grown up on it. Whatever it was, I still loved it.

Most nights, I would wake up to the sound of my mum crying and the ever-so-familiar smell of alcohol. Every second night, she was attempting suicide. Her method varied: sometimes it was overdosing on tablets that were prescribed to her or cutting her wrist with a knife. We kids had to take care of mum after these attempts. I hated endowment days — which was the name for what we call the pension today — because we knew that mum would buy beer, and we would have to be on suicide watch with her. She would play her country-and-western music, and one I remember clearly is 'Sea of Heartbreak' by Don Gibson. Whenever I hear this song it takes me back to the caravan.

She constantly had a bandage around her wrists. She'd get herself so worked up that she would often hyperventilate and have an epileptic fit. This traumatised me, seeing my mother falling to the ground, body thrashing about and her head smashing on the ground, all the while struggling for breath. I ran away from her when it happened. But not my youngest brother; he would be running towards Mum with a paper bag, which he'd hold over her face to help her get her breath back. It always worked. What a brave little boy.

We didn't stay there for long before my mum started a relationship with her sister's ex-husband. Shocking but true. They had a farmhouse that was surrounded by paddocks in the middle of nowhere, and the closest town was a tiny, dusty old place, 50 kilometres away.

Unbeknown to me at the time, this farm sat along the site of a massacre that happened by a river, the Brodribb River Massacre. As a group of Gunai/Kurnai mob bathed in the water, a group of white people on their horses attacked, killing some and maiming others of the tribal group. Of the survivors that day, a little boy was taken by one of the murderers, a stockman. The little boy had a tribal name and only spoke his language, so the stockman gave him his name: Charles Hammond. This little boy would grow to be a good stockman himself. This little boy was my great-great-great-grandfather. He met my great-great-great-grandmother, Hannah McCleod, on Country, and they would go on to have children. As a small child, she had been found by the water, further south in San Remo, with a group of her family, including elders. They were gathered up by the white people and made to walk on foot some hundreds of kilometres to Moody Yallock, where all my people were told to live. This area was unfamiliar to them, as it was not their Country. Hannah somehow escaped and travelled back to her Country, where she would later meet my great-great-great-grandfather. Her tribal name was Gallambuk. I have named my house after her.

CHAPTER 5

We would eventually move to that farm, but before we did, we were living in Orbost with my grandmother's first cousin, Uncle Freddie, who was like a brother to her. He lived there with his wife and kids. I saw a dead body for the first time in that house. I recall that one morning, all the adults in the house were crying and screaming from the bathroom. I looked inside and saw that a baby girl had drowned in the bathtub, which contained shallow water. She must have been about seven months old. The ambulance soon arrived, but by this time, my aunty was holding her lifeless baby on her lap, crying, in the lounge room of the house. At that time, I didn't really understand death; I just knew that I never saw that baby girl again. The adults drank for days and days after this. I also remember that, due to the amount of people and mouths to feed in this house, all we ate was rabbit stew every night. Uncle Freddie would catch rabbits, gut them in the backyard beside his shed, and then come and sit on the back steps and skin them. I would sit beside him, skinning the rabbits. Peeling the fur off the bony little animals. That was our thing; we bonded over it.

A few years later, I'd been sent to bed after being walloped over the backside for swearing. I was laying on the top bunk with my head facing the wall, crying, when I felt like someone was sitting beside me. My whole body froze; I tried to yell out but nothing would come out. I had an overwhelming sense of Uncle Freddie at that moment. Then I could hear myself screaming. My mum and siblings ran into my bedroom, and I leapt off the top bunk. I appeared to be hysterical, so my mum put me in a cold shower and my sister stayed in the bathroom with me. I kept repeating my uncle's name over and over. After getting out of the shower and sitting in the lounge room, explaining to my mum what had happened, there came a knock on the front door. There stood two police officers — I could hear talking but not exactly what was said. When Mum returned, she told us that the police had come to deliver a death message. My rabbit-skinning uncle had died.

So, we moved to the farm, and played happy family with my aunt's ex-husband, the father of my cousins. My oldest brother would set rabbit traps every night and check them in the morning. Sure enough, there would be rabbits, so that was our dinner most nights there as well. Rabbit stew. There were also horses at the farm, and we would ride them bare-back. This uncle and Mum were avid beer-drinkers. I had never known my uncle to be a violent man until he started drinking grog with my mum. This went on for a little while: the drinking and the fighting. Then one night, it became really violent, and Mum decided it was time to get out of this volatile relationship. Why she decided to do this in the middle of the night, in such an isolated area, is beyond me. Not to mention with four kids at her tail. But off we went, running through the paddocks, under and over barbed-wire fences. All of a sudden, I could hear my mother's name being called out over the revs of a car engine, and then I saw headlights smashing through the very same barbed-wire fences that we had just been through. *Oh my god, he is going to kill us.* We made it to a house that was on the highway, and Mum practically banged the door down, screaming for help. This house I saw every day; it sat on a hill close to the highway. It was red brick and seemed like a mansion to me. The gardens surrounding the house were a floral delight, with all colours of the rainbow. Now I felt so embarrassed, sitting in that nice house with a raving lunatic outside, and my mum drunk and carrying on. The police were called, and we were out of there. We went and stayed in Orbost for the night, and went back to the farmhouse the next day to get our clothes.

We ended up back in Morwell, where my grandparents were. But this time, we were homeless, so we had to live in an empty office block that had poor insulation and was freezing cold at night. Mum continued to drink alcohol, more so on endowment days. I knew that when I came home from school, she would be drunk. Most nights, usually after midnight, Mum would wake us kids up and tell us to get in the car. Then we'd drive through all the backstreets of this town to my aunt's house — Mum's sister — so Mum could get some cigarettes from her. You have no ideas how long it takes for a drunk driver to get from one end of town to the other, especially through the backstreets. It would be almost daylight before we would get back to our squat and go back to bed for a little while, then get up for school.

I would fret and cry for my dad every single night. I used to tell my mum to find my dad because I wanted to live with him. One night, when she was drunk, my mum grabbed me by my hair and smashed my head up against the brick wall, yelling at me to stop crying for my father. She made me want to leave even more! A few days after this incident was my eighth birthday. That day, Mum kept me home from school, and we went for a walk to the nearest phone box, which was on the main highway. I watched as she dialled some numbers and then spoke to someone on the other end. I heard her say, *come pick her up, I can't deal with her anymore*. Oh my god, the best birthday ever!

I wasn't sure what was said after that; I only heard what I wanted to hear, and everything after that was a blur. We walked back home, I packed my stuff up and waited. Days turned into weeks. During this waiting, my mum was still getting drunk with Aboriginal men. Then one day, all us kids were home when all of a sudden, my mum walked out of the office blocks and got into a car with a black man with frizzy hair and drove off. No goodbyes, no nothing. My little brother was running up the road as fast as he could, chasing after the car screaming out 'Mummy!' But that was that. She was gone. *Oh my god, what are we going to do?* We had no one. We knew our grandparents didn't want us, and we didn't know where our father was. Mind you, I was still waiting for the man to pick me up.

After what felt like a long time, we decided to go to our grandparents' house. I didn't want to go, because my grandparents never had any food in the house. As adults, I have asked my siblings to describe their childhood in one word. Their words were 'traumatising', 'terrifying', and 'sad'; mine was 'hungry'.

When we got there, my grandmother opened the door and asked us what we wanted. My big brother told her, and she said, 'Get in here, and don't muck up or I will call welfare and gungais to get rid of you.' My grandfather put us in a bedroom, shut the door, and told us not to come out. There was no light bulb, so it was complete darkness, and I was terrified of the dark. I would lie on the floor, looking at the light coming through the gap under the door, and cry to be let out. My siblings would tell me to come back to bed. All four of us slept in a single bed together, which was very uncomfortable.

Our grandparents used to keep their bread, butter, and jam in their bedroom, which they kept under lock and key. There were times when my brothers and sister would dare me to go knock on their bedroom door and ask for bread so we could eat. My grandmother would hand out a couple of slices of stale bread. I shared them with my brothers and sister. You have no idea how nice and tasty stale bread is when you're starving. I don't think they did this to be nasty; I believe that this is what they had to do back in the days on the mission, when they received rations.

My grandparents were also insomniacs — up all night and slept all day. Us kids were on a different sleeping pattern than they were, so we were up on our own and starving. We would open the oven to find a baking tray full of old cooking oil that had been sitting there for a long time, possibly years. We would scrape some of the fat, put it on the slices of bread, melt it by putting the bread covered with dripping in a pan, and then add salt. Dripping and salt. It was absolutely disgusting, but we ate it anyway. We had only been there a couple of nights when my grandmother loaded us all in their car with her and Grandad. We drove for hours until we reached Bendigo, where our Aunty Dot was at a teachers' college, training to be a teacher. My grandmother pulled her out of the college and told her that she had to come back to look after us kids.

I was so glad that Aunty Dot came back; she used to cook and care for us. When I say cook, she could only work with what she had — porridge. So, it was porridge, morning, noon, and night. You would think that I'd have been put off ever eating porridge ever again, but to this day, I still love it.

One night during this time there was a knock on the front door; when my grandfather opened the door, there stood two big, burly white policemen. They asked my grandfather for his name, and he told them. They said that they had a warrant for his arrest over an unpaid fine, and he had the choice of either paying for the fine or doing time in the local jail to pay it off. My grandfather said he didn't have the money, so they handcuffed him and walked him to the rear of their paddy wagon. When I saw this, I screamed and cried. My grandmother followed them out and gave them the money, which I remember being about 30 dollars. Thirty lousy dollars. The police uncuffed Grandad and let him go.

I also remember that we all had moonas in our hair during this time, so my grandmother poured kerosene over my head, cut my long hair short, and wrapped a cloth over my head, telling me I had to wear it all day and night. My scalp was burning and itching like hell. But I dared not take this cloth off for fear she would flog me. I think we'd been there for about a week or two when there was a knock on the front door. It was my dad! He told us kids to get in the car. Off we went, up the freeway to Queensland.

When I got older and had my children, I grew especially close to my grandmother, and I would drive with my children to Bung Yarnda to spend time with her. As soon as I got there, she would parade me around the mission like I was Elle bloody Macpherson or something, telling everybody, *this is my granddaughter*. It was during one of these walks that I asked Nanny why she never had any children to Grandad, and she told me that immediately after she gave birth to my father, the hospital had sterilised her without her consent. At that time, this was done not only to Aboriginal unwed mothers but to white ones, too. She told me that she had never ever told my grandfather; he thought that *he* couldn't have any children. Can you imagine, living a lie for nearly 50 years of marriage? But my grandmother was the strongest and most resilient woman I had ever known. She taught me the valuable lesson of never playing the victim or feeling sorry for yourself. I think this is where I get my traits from. It's lucky I got something from her and not Grandad, or I would be walking around with 20 or so bloody mangy cats.

So, after what seemed like forever, we arrived in this dusty mining town in central Queensland, Mt Isa, where we ended up living with my dad and his new girlfriend. I got on with her well. I didn't care where I was, as long I was with my dad. I felt safe with him. I knew there was not going to be any more alcohol, violence, and hunger. And there were huge pawpaw trees in the backyard.

My brothers and sister didn't like Dad's girlfriend, though, and made it known. They played up something shocking. They would say to her, when Dad was not around, 'You're not our mother; you can't tell us what to do.' This caused a bit of friction in Dad's relationship. Our house had ducted air conditioning, with vents on the floor, so every time Dad and the girlfriend argued — and they did so in the bedroom so that we wouldn't hear — us kids would lie down on the floor with our ears to the vent. We heard every word. Their relationship didn't last long;

one day, while she was at work, my dad came home in a mad dash and told us to quickly pack and get into the car.

Off we went again, back on the highway, back to Victoria.

CHAPTER 6

Back in Victoria, my dad rented a one-bedroom flat in Morwell and got a job as manager of the Aboriginal Co-op. He was the boss man. My brothers and sister didn't stay there long; I can't remember now why they left, but they went to live with Mum. By then, our mum was living in Wellington, New South Wales, with an Aboriginal church minister; his son was in the Manly rugby league team at the time. Mum had also turned Christian, but this was *after* she'd ended up in jail for doing a break-and-enter at an electrical store, with the frizzy-haired black man she'd taken off with. The next school holiday, my brothers and sister rang me, telling me that I should come and see Mum, and that I'd be okay, as she wasn't drinking alcohol anymore. So, I went up there for the holidays. It was good to see her. She looked different. My siblings had failed to mention that my mother was also in a relationship with this minister, though, who had kids of his own.

Soon after arriving, my brothers, and two of the minister's sons, and I — all being musically inclined — realised that we were Australia's answer to The Jackson Five. Well, maybe not Australia, but regional New South Wales, at least. We would sing and dance to their music. My sister wasn't included, as she was tone-deaf, and couldn't dance to save her life. She did play a vital part in our performance, though: she was the 'stop', 'play,' and 'rewind' girl for the tape recorder. She was even our announcer when we decided to perform for Mum and the minister. Mum liked it, but the minister thought it was the devil's work and put a swift end to our impending stardom. I didn't like him, but true to my siblings' words, Mum was no longer drinking alcohol and was attending church regularly. We ended up going to church with her, and even painted the church while I was there. I enjoyed my time with her; it felt like I was getting to know who my mum was for the first time in my life. I had never seen her sober for so long before. This mum I truly loved being around. She was caring, affectionate, funny, loving: the best mother a little girl could ask for.

I missed living with my brothers and sister. Being a family. Yeah, we fought, but what brothers and sisters don't? All I knew was that they were still living with Mum, and I was an only child with Dad. A very spoilt only child. I got what I wanted whenever I wanted. In saying that, I was only nine, and I was ironing my dad's work clothes and cooking dinner for the two of us. They weren't flash meals, but they were good, considering my age. My favourite meal to cook was steak and veggies. My dad was a great cook and made delicious meals for us when he cooked. Most of them were one-pot wonders. I never ate onions — couldn't stand the taste or the smell of them — so most times, my dad would make two pots, one with onion, one without.

On paydays, my dad was so busy that he'd give me a heap of cash and tell me to go food shopping. Most nights, my father would go to the local pub, and I would be home on my own. By ten at night, I would start getting a bit frightened, so I would run to the pub and go in to get him. His mates would say, 'Oh, your boss is here, you have to go home.' Some nights, we would get pizza on the way home. Our flat was right next door to the Lionel Rose hostel. This is where Aunty Dot was living and working, which was just as well. She was the only female in my life during this time that resembled a mother to me. I loved her so much as a child; actually, I still do. I have so much respect for her. One morning when I was eleven, I woke up and was bleeding from my nether regions. I didn't know what was happening. I thought I was dying or something. I went to the toilet and just sat there crying. I cried out for my dad and told him what was happening; he pulled the sheet off his bed and said, 'Put this between your legs, I'll be back soon. Don't move.' A few minutes later, Aunty Dot arrived with my father, and gave me a pad and told me to shower. She explained to me why I was bleeding. That day, my dad and I went shopping, and he bought every brand of pads in the supermarket.

My brothers and sister would take turns coming to live or stay with Dad and me. They never stayed for long, but I loved seeing them. Then came the time when Dad and I went on a road trip. He told me that we were going to my mum's place in New South Wales to pick up my sister. When we got there, he went to the boot of the vehicle, grabbed some bags, and gave them to my brother. Then he said he was going to the shop, and asked me if I wanted anything from there. I was a kid — of course I did. So, I ordered up: *a can of Coke and a packet of chips, Samboy chips, please*. Dad said okay, and that he would be back soon. Four bloody weeks later, no Coke, no chips! The man had left me with my mother in her new house. She was no longer living with the minister and his kids, but she had her own housing-commission house with my brothers and sister. It was a nice weatherboard home with three bedrooms. The furniture wasn't flash, but it was my mum's, and, as usual, she kept the house spotless. The only problem was, she was back on the grog. The first night she got drunk, she started on me. She asked me why I'd been living with my father and not her. She said that he wasn't my real father anyway, and that I should be living with her. She told me the name of my alleged real father. A name I had never heard before. That was it — I spent the rest of my time with her sitting on her kitchen bench, looking out the window, which had a good view of the road leading to her house. I was looking out for my dad's car.

When I was finally reunited with my dad, I told him what she said to me. He told me that when my older brother and sister were young, and I was not yet born, my mother had left him. She'd also left the kids with him. My dad said he was struggling, so he went and looked for Mum and found her at her sister's house, with another man. She went back to Dad and the kids, and when they argued, while boozed up, she would try to hurt Dad by saying that she was pregnant before she came back, and it was to the other man. My dad and I have often spoken about getting a DNA test to disprove her, but what's the point. I look like my dad and I have his ways.

That was the turning point for me, though. I decided then and there that I was not going to see my mother anymore. She had hurt me and my dad in her attempts to separate us, and all to try and get me to live with her. My mother then began to make phone calls while she was drunk, yelling at me on the phone, 'He's not your dad!' I would hang up on her. Sometimes Mum would threaten to kill herself if I didn't come see her. I would be crying and begging her not to harm herself. It got to a point that my dad and I took the phone off the hook at night.

It was some time before I saw her again. She'd send the other kids down to Victoria from New South Wales with messages for me, saying that she loved and missed me. I never doubted that she loved me — what mother wouldn't love their child? I just think that she resented the fact that my dad left her, and that I'd never hated him for it or spoken badly about him with her or to her. All I ever wanted was to be a bloody kid and enjoy my childhood. But whenever I spoke to her or saw her, it became like a game of tug of war. *I'm better than him, I've suffered, he left me, and so you should be living with me.*

After a few messages from my siblings, I decided to go and see Mum during the school break. I caught the V/Line train from Melbourne to Sydney because she was living in Sydney with a new man. I contacted her prior to leaving and made her promise not to drink a drop of alcohol while I was with her. I was only going to be there for a week — how hard could it be to stay sober for that length of time? She made this promise, but she must have had her eyes, fingers, and toes crossed, because she didn't keep her word.

The train was a night-time service, so I slept all the way, woke up, and was in Sydney. That first night, Mum got on the piss and started the verbal abuse, calling me a little black bitch. The next morning, I rang my dad. He wired me some money, and I booked my fare for the train trip back to Melbourne.

These trips continued, same ole, same ole. Promises, promises. I'd had enough. All those times I was sitting in the smoke-filled carriages of the interstate train or on the Greyhound buses, I never saw any other kids of my age travelling on their own. If I saw kids, they were with their families. I was a shy kid, but I had street smarts, if that makes sense. From an early age, I had an instinct about who to trust and who to stay clear away from.

On one of my last trips to Sydney to see Mum, as a child, it was her payday and she went food shopping. But she never came home; instead, she went to the pub for happy hour, along with the shopping. Meat and all. This didn't bother her. Her boyfriend staggered into the house at some ungodly hour on his own, and I asked where Mum was. He said, 'The crazy bitch is still at the pub,' and that she wouldn't come home with him. My instincts told me to get out — *don't stay in the house alone with this man* — so I went out the front door, umbrella in hand for protection. Through the western suburbs of Sydney, not yet a teenager, I was running as fast as I could to retrieve my mother. I wanted her to come home; I was so tired. I just wanted to sleep. And I wasn't going to sleep unless she was there, drunk or not. Mind you, I didn't know where Mum went to do her shopping, but I knew where the pub was. I finally got there and could see her through the window. She was laughing it up, a schooner in one hand and a pool cue in the other. What a glorious time she was having. I'd just run for dear life, and she was having a ball. I walked in the pub, gave her a tap with the umbrella, and told her to get home. Must say, it was a slow walk home. Silence is golden.

When we got to the house, she barged through the door and headed straight to her room. I went to the spare bedroom and got into bed, clothes and all. I never put my PJs on — I was smarter than that. You always had to be on the ready. Then I heard the fighting — arguing and the sounds of slapping and then crying. While this was happening, I shoved the wardrobe up against the door. Then I made a bed on the floor, next to this furniture, to add reinforcement so that no one could get into the room. The next morning, I was expecting bruises and a war zone but no, Mum was in the kitchen, making a hot breakfast, and appeared to be happy. Like everything was normal. I had to get out of there, quick smart.

I don't remember my brothers or sister being at Mum's when I visited. I think Mum and Dad did a swap, a 'three-for-one' deal. I used to wish that they'd stay there when I visited. I did hear their stories of living with Mum through telephone conversations. One story in particular, told by my little brother, still breaks my heart. He would spend most of his nights not tucked in a warm bed, preparing for school for the next day, but closely following Mum as she walked the streets, from pub to pub. He'd sit outside the pub for hours just to keep an eye on her. When she was being followed by my little brother, she never knew, and when they reached home, which was on the second level, she'd stagger upstairs and my brother would climb the brick wall to get inside the window he'd left ajar for his return home. He'd get into bed when he heard her come in the front door. *Oh, my goodness, I thought I had it bad when I visited.* This poor little boy; I felt so hurt and sad when he told me this. He was subjected to this shit most nights. Whenever I heard these stories, I wished that I could have traded places with them. It wasn't fair that he had to go through this, and I never did.

CHAPTER 7

If Mum taught me anything in the short time that I lived with her — and the even shorter visits during my juvenile years — it was morals and manners. She drummed into us that we should never hate anybody. I carry these values with me to this day. And it might explain why I don't have hatred for my mum; I love her dearly. I've come to understand her a lot more. During those days, I believe my mother was going through a nervous breakdown and suffering depression, due to the separation of her and Dad, and the stress of being left with four children to feed. No support and no one to talk to. So, I don't hate my mum — I just feel a sad kind of love. Years later my mother apologised for her treatment of me, an apology I have accepted. I actually thanked her for being a bad mother; it was because of her that I became a good mother, everything she wasn't. And the other kids could have left her and come and lived with Dad and me any time if they wanted, but I think they felt sorry for her and some form of loyalty towards her.

I had started high school by now. I was a goofy little black kid, big feet, shoes that were too small for me but looked good and, wait for it, little bloody fripples but no bra. *We've got a problem.* I spoke to Aunty Dot about the no-bra situation, and she told Dad that I needed one. He'd had no idea. He gave me some money, and I went to the shops to buy my very first bra. What a moment. I ended up buying a training bra as the sales assistant suggested. I wore it day and night. And as shameful as this might sound, it was the only bra I had until I was 16 years old. I was busting out of the seams. I'm surprised that little bra held together as long as it did.

So there I was, bleeding from places I never knew bled, my chest was growing, and I was getting hair. *What the hell is going on? I need a mother!* I couldn't tell Dad too much; he was hardly ever home anyway, as his job required him to travel a lot. During those times, I would stay with Aunty Dot. Sometimes I'd go with Dad, at least until the time he went to a pub in Fitzroy and told me to wait in the car — which I didn't, as I needed to go to the toilet, forgive me — and I accidentally locked the keys in the car. Oh shit, didn't he go off. He was lucky I hadn't driven off in the friggin' car and left him there. Needless to say, I wasn't allowed to go with him for a while. This suited me, because by now I had formed friendships at school. This was about the time the movie *Grease*, starring John Travolta and Olivia Newton-John, was a hit. In the movie, there was a group of girls called the 'Pink Ladies', and they all wore identical pink jackets. Well, my friends and I formed a similar group, but we couldn't afford the jackets, so we just wore pink jumpers, and, to add spruce and character, we put our names on the front in large black print. If you had a boyfriend, you'd put his name on the back. I had a boyfriend — an Italian boy, Gino — and I had his name on the back of my jumper. I was pretty cool. I didn't know what it meant to have a boyfriend, because I was so young and dopey. But we just hung out; he was my best mate, and we would dink each other around on his bike. Years later, I was reading the local newspaper and saw his name in the obituary section, commemorating ten years since he'd died in a car accident in Queensland.

Role-playing as the cast members of *Grease* wasn't all my friends and I were doing. Every Friday night, we hung out at the newly built shopping centre in town. It was there I started smoking cigarettes and stealing clothes. The fashion during these times was skin-tight bubblegum jeans. I would never have dared to ask my dad for the money for these jeans; they were so expensive. So, during one of our Friday-night hang-outs, my friends and I decided that we all wanted bubblegum jeans from Just Jeans. There were three of us, and there were three change rooms in this particular shop. We were all wearing baggy jeans, so that after we put the bubblegums on, we could just walk out of the store with two pairs of jeans on. Easy, simple — this was my ingenious idea. So, we walked in, pretending we didn't know each other. I grabbed my jeans and set the plan in motion. I entered the dressing-room, and quickly took my baggy jeans off, put the skinnies on, and then my jeans back on over the top. Done! I walked out of the dressing room and started looking at other clothes. I was terrified to walk out of the store; I thought that I would get caught. My heart was pounding so fast. I was waiting for my friends to finish in their change rooms. When they came out, we started to leave, but the shop assistant walked to the doorway as we were about to exit. 'Stay there until the police get here,' she said. 'I know you have stolen jeans on.' Somehow, I managed to get out of the store unnoticed. Once outside, I ran all the way home. I felt bad that they'd been caught and I hadn't. So much so, I never wore the bubblegums in front of them, and I never stole from shops again.

I wasn't the only one making new friends — my dad had also met a new lady friend. She was a social worker who worked with troubled children. *Wait until she met me.* I really liked her, though. She had a lot of time for me. She took me swimming and bushwalking, things that I had never done before. She and Dad were a loving couple, and she made him so happy. She came to watch me play netball and basketball and cheer me on. She also encouraged Dad to get active, as she was into healthy foods and fitness. Next thing you know, he was umpiring Aussie Rules football and running long distance during his spare time to keep fit. Problem with this was that he would make me run with him. I don't know why — I wasn't umpiring. It was fun, though. We'd be running, and you could hear my dad puffing and panting a mile away, while I'd be easily running next to him talking nonstop. Those were the days. I was probably the fittest black kid in town.

My dad and his new lady friend decided to live together, so we moved out of our flat and into a house in another part of town. For the first time in a long time, I had my own room and my own space. I don't think that the other kids ever came to that house, except for my older brother. I was in bed sleeping in one morning, home on my own, when I heard a knock on the front door. I got out of bed to open the door, but no one was there, so I went back to bed. All of a sudden, I could hear the sounds of someone climbing through the front window and into the lounge room. I grabbed my dad's cricket bat and ran to the front window, ready to take a swing, when a head came through first. *Hang on a minute, this head looks familiar.* It was my oldest brother. He's lucky I had good observation skills. I swore at him, and said, 'Why you can't come in the front door like everybody else?' He told me that he'd knocked, but no one answered, and he thought no one was home. Talk about impatient, and so much for Neighbourhood Watch. When he got in, he asked me if we had any alfoil. I went to the kitchen and came back with it. I was thinking — *what does he need this for?* — but I got it anyway. When I went back into the lounge room, there he was, and sitting in front of him was all this green leafy stuff that stunk the house out. I asked what it was, and he said, 'Yarndi.' He said he needed my help. He was grabbing piles of this green leafy stuff, and told me to wrap them tightly in the alfoil. It turns out, I was aiding and abetting a bloody drug dealer. So once all the foils were wrapped, and there was no more yarndi, he headed off, saying, 'See ya later.' Whatever. He came back later that night, though, and gave me some money; he said it was for helping him. When I saw the amount of money, I said, 'Well, let me know if you need any more help.' That was my first encounter with marijuana. There would be many more to follow.

My father's brother had also met someone, and they were getting married. She was heavily pregnant on her wedding day — I think they were trying to do the right thing by choosing to marry. I didn't understand, though, because prior to them getting married, I saw so much violence between them. He would punch her with a closed fist, right to the face, and most of the time, she was busted up. We all got dressed up: my grandmother wore a hot-pink dress with a hat to match, and my grandfather was all dolled up in a fancy suit. It was the first time I had seen them dress so well. Actually, it was the first wedding I had ever been to.

When they were planning the wedding, it became a family affair. I thought for sure that I was going to be in the bridal party.

I was a cute little girl. Who wouldn't want me in their wedding? As it turns out, them. I was shitty throughout the whole ceremony. So, they were married, and off we all went to the hall, which was right next to the church in Yallourn North, where they were having their reception. There was heaps of food, but we couldn't start eating, apparently, until the speeches were made. I was famished, and learning quickly that people talk so much shit at weddings. Well, for the first speech, my uncle got up and went to open his mouth, and then his new wife went into labour. Off we went to the hospital. We sat around for hours and hours, and I never got to eat. She had a healthy baby boy. Kisses all round, and then we trotted off to the local pub. I'm not yet twelve and there I was, dancing like nobody's business on the dance floor until the wee hours of the night. That was the highlight of the wedding but for some reason, call me crazy, the rest of it put me off ever getting married and having kids. This newly married couple were the biggest potheads I have ever met, and the violence continued. Still, they remained married for some time, and had four more children. They were such bad parents, though, that they didn't raise any of them. Her mum and dad intervened, took the kids away from them, and raised them until they were adults.

Whenever I went to their house, there was always the pungent smell of marijuana. It was overpowering. They smoked dope all day, every day, in their main bedroom. People would come and go all day; they'd enter the room and leave soon after. It didn't take a genius to work out that they were also dealing. In Victoria at this time, the police had a drug campaign, 'Operation Noah', whereby members of the public could call a hotline and remain anonymous to dob in a drug dealer. Well, this was my favourite time of the year. Whenever I visited their house during this operation, I'd threaten to dob them in. They'd call me the little gungai, which means 'police' in my language. I never did make that call. I was only gammin.

The only reason I was frequenting the drug house was because we had a band, and I was singing in it. We had rehearsals at the house, and we'd try and get gigs. Our band got a bit of attention as we were all related: my brothers, my uncle, and then there was me — a skinny little kid. There was one time when we got a gig at a bikie's convention set in the hills of country Victoria. I think it was their clubhouse. I was scared, as I had heard bad things about them, but once we were there, I sang, got paid, and then we left. Job done, and they weren't so bad after all. I'll just say that they do know how to party.

A few months after the wedding, Dad and his lady friend decided to move to Alice Springs. I didn't know why, but thinking back now, she must have got a transfer with her job. She left a few weeks before Dad and me, while we packed the house up. During this time, I was whinging and moaning to Dad. I didn't want to move and leave my Italian boyfriend or my friends. Before I left, I hatched a plan with all my friends. Another ingenious plan. I told my friends that when I got there, I'd send them my address, so that they could send me money. Once I had enough money, I'd buy a train ticket back to Victoria. I also told my dad that he shouldn't bother about enrolling me in the school up there because I wasn't going to go anyway. He just ignored me.

When it was time to leave, my dad and I were going to drive to Adelaide, and then catch the train from Adelaide to Alice Springs. We went to say goodbye to my grandparents. It was sad leaving them; my little brother was there, too, but he didn't want to come with us. That was the hardest part — leaving him, not knowing when I would see him again. We took a family photo, and got in the car for our drive to Adelaide. When we got to Adelaide, we drove straight to the railway station, where we didn't have to wait long. When the train arrived, we boarded, and there we stayed for days and days. It felt like a lifetime. I had so many questions: *what's it like in Alice Springs? Where is Alice Springs? What will we do there?* I have never eaten so many meat pies in all my days.

Finally, we arrived. *What an eyesore.* The town was covered in red dirt; it was dusty and hot. As the train pulled up at the platform, I could see my dad's lady friend waiting for us. We had to wait for the car to get off the freight train, which was attached to the passenger train. Once it was off, we got in the car, and drove to our new house. It was a really nice brick home on one of the main roads of the Alice. It had air conditioning and three big bedrooms. It was the flashiest house that I had lived in. For a brief minute, I thought that I might just give it a go in my new environment, but then it was my first day at my new school, and, as an act of defiance, I decided to wear my old school uniform. Not just that, I also decided to wear the coat that had my favourite Carlton Football Club footy player's name and number at the rear. This big knee-length dark-blue duffle coat. My dad told me not to, as I looked bloody ridiculous. But I showed him. *Send me to a new school and this is what you'll get.* Talk about sweat, though — I was so hot in this coat, which clearly didn't suit the Alice Springs climate. I wore it for about three or four days. When I met new people at the school, they asked if I was coloured. I wasn't sure entirely what this meant but had an idea it was something other than white. So I replied, 'Yes.' And when I was asked the whereabouts of my mother, I'd say she'd died of breast cancer. It was easier than the truth.

Dad got a high-profile job with the Department of Aboriginal Affairs. Again, this job required him to travel, but he was only travelling within the Territory, to remote Aboriginal stations. Yuendumu, Hermannsburg, and other similar places. On a few occasions, I went with him. It would take hours to get anything remotely close to civilisation. The landscape was desolated and barren, with red dirt for miles and miles, and the heat was unbearable. During these drives, I was worried about breaking down. I would worry if we had enough water and food to survive. The road we were travelling on was so remote, and there wasn't another vehicle for miles. Well, I never saw another vehicle during our whole trips. As we got closer to our destinations, there were communities living on the outskirts; their homes were humpies. It was a real eye-opener for me. My dad was like a tour guide, stopping along the way to point out large anthills and the flora of this grand landscape. These trips were so educational from a cultural perspective. I was amazed that my people were still living the traditional ways and still had language. We would stay the night in makeshift rooms — fitted with air conditioners, thank goodness — and feast on kangaroo on a spit.

CHAPTER 8

About the time I was living in Central Australia with my father, my little brother was living with our mother in Sydney. They'd arrived there by train from Wellington. The train trip was an overnight one. They knew nobody in Sydney, but headed towards the suburb of Redfern, which they knew was highly populated with Aboriginal people. All they had were the clothes on their backs. They got to a park and saw a group of Aboriginal people sitting around, drinking alcohol. Mum walked up to them, introduced herself, and sat there for three days and three nights, drinking with her new-found friends. My brother stayed awake the whole time, keeping an eye on Mum. Protecting her. After this drinking binge, Mum decided it was time to sort her life out and get help, but, still homeless, she and my brother squatted in an abandoned warehouse, a derelict building, huddling in a corner to keep warm. Mum telephoned the prominent Mr Perkins, who was a friend of my father, and explained her circumstances to him. By the end of the day she was offered emergency housing in the Western suburbs. A two-bedroom house with no furnishings; Mum rang Salvation Army and every other support agency for assistance with furniture and food. By the end of the day, Mum and my brother had five beds, three televisions, and two fridges. Every time someone would come to the house, my brother hid the food so that they could get more.

A few months passed, and Mum and my brother were going really well. Mum was still drinking alcohol, but there was no violence — until her ex-boyfriend was released from jail. They got back together, and he moved into the house with them. The fighting was worse when they were drinking grog. On one occasion, while he was punching Mum around the head, my brother got out of bed and crash-tackled him. This only made him madder, and he lashed out at Mum more. Mum had had enough, and she grabbed a knife and stabbed him in the gut. As Mum put the knife in him, he stopped what he was doing and looked at her, stunned and shocked. Mum pulled the handle out, expecting to see blood, but all she saw was a bent blade. The knife was an old butter knife.

On another occasion, it got so bad that my mum and brother had to leave the house and seek refuge at a friend's house. During the night, in the early hours, my brother got out of bed to get a drink of water. As he was in the kitchen, the ex-boyfriend was at the front of Mum's friend's house, and threw a brick through the window. The brick landed on the bed where my brother had been sleeping just moments before. Shattered glass everywhere. They called the police, but by the time they arrived, he was nowhere to be seen.

I turned 13 years old. My dad threw a big party for me with all my new friends. I even got presents in the mail from my long-distant family members. It was probably my second-best birthday ever. That was also the night I first discovered drinking alcohol. I got drunk on beer. I hated the taste of it, but that's all that was on offer from my friends, so beer it was. Not long after, I got more mail. It was an envelope, and inside was a heap of money. I think there was about seventy-five dollars, if memory serves me correctly, and a letter signed by all the friends I had left behind in Victoria. I had forgotten about them sending me money up. I didn't use this money to go back to Victoria, though — instead, I kept it for tuckshop at school. I didn't have the heart to inform my Victorian friends that I'd made new friends in Alice Springs and that I was loving it there.

I started playing basketball for a local team and was selected to represent Alice Springs. This meant that I got to travel to Darwin to try out for the Northern Territory team. I got to stay in a flash hotel as well. I was a good basketball player; I was quick and could shoot baskets. So it was no surprise I was told that I would definitely make the NT squad. However, due to my very competitive nature, I ended up with five fouls, which meant I got sent off for the remainder of the game. By getting sent off, I also limited my chances of being selected. I never made the squad. I was devastated, but I took it on the chin.

When I returned from Darwin, a new girl had started school and was in my classes. She was from England, and had a proper English accent and the palest skin I've ever seen on a person. She was living at the local caravan park with her dad, who was a lot older than my father. He was even older than my grandfather. It turns out that her mum had not long died, and they had moved to Australia for a fresh start. My new friend was a vegetarian, the first vegetarian I had ever met. Prior to meeting her I didn't even know what a vegetarian was. She would often stay at my house, and every time she did, I would cook us mashed potato and baked beans for dinner. Not much cooking involved, though.

It was approaching Christmas in 1984, and Dad decided we were going to Victoria for the holidays. I was excited about this; I couldn't wait to see my family. Better yet, I found out that we were having a big Christmas, and my brothers and sister were going to be there. I hadn't seen them for so long. With all the talk about my upcoming Christmas, I felt sorry for my friend, who had no family other than her dad, so I asked her if she wanted to come with us. This way, she would get to see Australia as well. She asked her dad and I asked mine. They both agreed, and she came to Victoria with us. Must have been a cultural shock for her, having her first Christmas in Australia with an Aboriginal family.

After we came back to the Alice, my dad's lady friend had to return to Melbourne, as she'd heard that her elderly mother was missing, and she went down to help with the search. About three days later, while she was staying at the family home, her mother's whereabouts still unknown, she went under the house where they stored old furniture and other things. I think she was looking for photo albums. When she was down there, she found her mother. She was lifeless. She had suicided with a heap of tablets. My dad flew straight down, leaving me in Alice Springs. I told him that I would stay with my English friend at the caravan park, but I didn't. I stayed home on my own.

That coming weekend I had a basketball game, which kept me occupied. The night before my game, I went to the caravan park to hang with my friend. As I was walking to her caravan, I saw the best tracksuit hanging on the communal clothes line. It was yellow, which I thought would really suit my complexion. So I grabbed it off the line, and went and saw my friend. This is called 'snow-dropping'. I told her what I had done, and didn't think much more about it. The next night I had my big basketball game, and I wanted to step out in style with my new tracksuit on. Midway through my game, as I was dribbling the ball and preparing for a layup, I could see two police officers walking into the stadium. They walked towards my coach, and next thing, the whistle blew, and my coach was signalling for me to come off the court. The police wanted to talk to me about a stolen tracksuit. I tried to lie and say that I didn't know what they were talking about. But there it was, sitting on top of my bag, which was on the bleachers. So, I handed it to them, and they led me out of the stadium and into the police vehicle. They wanted to escort me home and speak to my parent; only, of course, my parent was in another state and I was on my own. I had to come up with something quickly. When we got to my house, they asked to speak to my father. I went inside, came straight back out, and said, 'Oh, that's right, he's at the casino. He'll be back later.' They left, not another word said. I knew that my friend must have dobbed me in to the cops. I never spoke to her again.

Often, during my lunchbreaks at school, I would hear music coming from a rehearsal room. I could hear music but no vocals. One day, I plucked up the courage to go in. Inside were a music teacher and some boys, all with instruments in their hands. They were playing 'Walking on Sunshine'. I grabbed the microphone from the stand and started singing, as I was familiar with the song. From then on, I was in the school rock band. Soon after I joined, we started to do lunchtime gigs in the school auditorium. It would be packed with students of all ages. I got on really well with the music teacher, and told him I wanted to learn the guitar, so he offered me guitar lessons after school and on weekends. My dad paid for these lessons, and would drop me off at the teacher's house. I started to learn piano as well. My dad was so encouraging.

Before Dad went to Melbourne to offer support, he and his lady friend had purchased a three-bedroom house with an in-ground pool. They were waiting for the property to settle. It was exciting, planning with her and Dad what we were going to do with the house. They told me I could paint my new room whatever colour I wanted. I couldn't wait to swim in the pool.

But when they got back from Melbourne, all their problems started. She cried all the time and stayed in bed a lot. I think she became depressed after the death of her mother. They had been really close, and she must have been missing her so much. Shortly after, she and Dad split up and we moved out. My dad went and stayed in a men's hostel, right in the middle of the town. It wasn't far from my dad's work but was a fair distance from my school. I wanted to stay with Dad, but the hostel was for men only. So we arranged for me to stay with a white family that lived close to my school. I would borrow my friend's pushbike and ride to the men's hostel every afternoon to see my dad. On my first visit, I noticed that the hostel was called Skid Row, which was an appropriate name. All the other residents at the hostel appeared to be down on their luck: homeless, jobless, and society's drop outs. Every time I went there, Dad and I would just go straight into his bedroom and talk.

Dad didn't seem to be himself. I could tell that he was lost. He told me he didn't want me around the other men that were staying there, which is why we stayed in his room. One of the other rooms had a television in it, though, and I wanted to watch TV because during my visits, my favourite show was on. His bedroom was just a single bed and a built-in wardrobe. A far cry from where he had come from. I hated leaving my dad there: I pretty much cried all the way back. After a few weeks, I couldn't do it anymore. I packed my bags up, went to visit Dad at the hostel, and I never left. I would have to sneak in and out, as the residents were strictly advised that 'under no circumstances were females allowed'.

During this time, my dad had to do a business trip to Melbourne. When he came back, he had a spring in his step and seemed to be smiling more. One night after work, we both snuck out of the hostel and walked to the phonebox. He made a phone call, and told me to come and say hello to the person on the other end. I did, and a female voice said 'Hello' back. I gave the phone back to Dad and waited for him to end the conversation. I wanted to know who it was. Finally, he ended the call, and told me that she was his new girlfriend, and that we were moving to Melbourne so that he could be with her. I told him I was not leaving the Alice, and if he made me move, I would quit school. He just ignored me again.

The bus trip was a long one. We drove through many towns and states before we arrived at the bus depot at Spencer Street railway station. As we exited the bus, I saw my oldest brother waiting for us. For a minute, I was happy again; I told my dad that I wanted to go stay with my brother until he got settled in Melbourne, and Dad agreed. So, it was hugs and kisses all round, and then my brother and I had to run to make the country-bound train departing any minute from Platform 1. My dad called out to me, 'Keep in touch.' Yeah, yeah. Almost three hours later, and after another sleep, we arrived in Morwell. During the final moments on the train, my brother told me that he was staying at a house with a woman that he had been seeing for a little while. He also told me that she was Aboriginal, from Mildura, in the north of Victoria. A far distance from where we were.

We got off the train and caught a taxi to the other end of town. I had to pay for the taxi fare with money that Dad had given me to keep me going. This house was full of strange Aboriginal people that I didn't know; there were no other children, just adults. I didn't know it yet, but what happened in this house was going to change me forever.

CHAPTER 9

The house reeked of stale alcohol, as if it had been spilt on the carpet and not cleaned. The house appeared bare of furniture; it reminded me of a typical drunken house. I noticed a vehicle in the driveway, an old Ford, but didn't know who it belonged to. As I climbed the many steps to enter the house, I saw an older woman standing at the front door with a big smile. My brother said, 'That's her, that's my girlfriend.' I thought that she must be a lot older than him.

It would soon be night, and the house was abuzz with people coming and going, all drinking alcohol. Beer and moselle were the drinks for the night. I didn't want to be there; I didn't feel safe. Then my brother's new girlfriend offered me a can of beer, saying to my brother, 'She'll be right.' My brother didn't say anything, so we took this as, 'Let her have a beer.' Well, one beer turned into many more while John Fogerty was on high volume on the little stereo. I was so drunk, but I remember that at the end of the night, a single mattress was put on the lounge-room floor and made up with a sheet and a blanket. My brother and his girlfriend were in their bedroom, which was up the hallway, the first bedroom on the left, opposite the only toilet in the house.

When I finally lay down, it didn't take me long to drift off to sleep. During the night, I went to roll over to my side, but felt pressure on my chest and I couldn't breathe. I tried to move, but could feel someone sitting on my chest, with their knees on my arms to prevent me from moving. My arms were aching, and my hands felt numb from a loss of circulation. I was trying to thrash my body to get him off but I couldn't move. I was pinned down. This man had his penis in my mouth, I was trying so hard to spit it out or bite on it. It was right at the back of my throat. I was choking. I felt smothered. I could also feel that my legs were spread wide apart, and there was another man on top of me, forcing his penis into me. It hurt so much. The pain was unbearable; there was a burning sensation. I couldn't scream for help; I felt helpless. Through the moonlight, I recognised the man between my legs as one of the men who had been drinking at the house earlier in the night. He was the cousin of my brother's girlfriend; I didn't recognise the man in my mouth. I shut my eyes so tight, I must have blacked out for a minute or two, because when I came to, they were getting off me, and then I heard footsteps, and the front door shut, and then a car started its engine. I heard the car reverse down the driveway and screech off.

It was still dark in the lounge room. I couldn't move, I was terrified. I didn't know what to do. I lay there awake for the rest of the night, just looking around. The sheets felt cold and damp, I thought it must have been sweat from my body, sweat from thrashing my body on the mattress. As soon as I saw the sunlight through the lounge-room window, I got up. It was then I saw that the sheet that I was lying on was covered in blood. I ripped the sheet off and was walking to the laundry with it when my brother's girlfriend opened their bedroom door. She looked at what I had in my hands and must have seen the blood on the sheets. She said to me, 'You better hide that, so your brother doesn't see it.' I wanted my brother to see it; I wanted to tell my brother what had happened.

That day I was so sore; I had pain in my stomach and couldn't eat. My throat was so sore. I wanted to tell someone, but I never. I found out later that the other man was the brother of my brother's girlfriend. He was her oldest brother, in his late thirties. It would be five years before I told my father. When I told him, he was driving the car on a busy Melbourne street and I was in the passenger seat. I don't know why I told him then, but something made me. I was so scared that he wouldn't believe me. He pulled the car over and cried. He wanted to know who they were, and to know everything that had happened. I felt so relieved. I had finally told someone and not just anybody — my father. It felt like a weight off my shoulders, and I could finally breathe again.

There are many reasons people don't report rapes or sexual assaults to police, or tell a friend or family, and these reasons differ. Some may be ashamed, some may think that people won't believe them, and some won't report it because of fear, and sometimes because of threats made by the rapist. My reason was that I blamed myself. Hours before my rape, I'd gone to the toilet and shut the door, but I couldn't lock it as it didn't have a lock. I sat on the toilet and tried to pee really fast before anybody could walk in on me. Someone did, but it was no accident. One of the rapists came in; he grabbed my hair with one hand, and grabbed my face, and forced his penis into my mouth. He was pushing it in and out of my mouth. I tried to get up, to get out of the toilet, but I couldn't. I forced myself to stand up, and I pushed past him and walked back into the lounge room, where everybody else was, including my brother. I sat on the lounge, frozen. I wanted to tell my brother so much, but I was worried about the outcome. I thought he would kill him. I was also in shock; I couldn't believe what had just happened. This is the reason I didn't and, after thirty-odd years, still haven't reported it.

I had always had pride in my appearance, and colour-coordinated my clothing with my shoes. My hair would be tied up neatly in a ponytail or a plait. After the rape, I didn't care. I stopped wearing all my nice clothes and asked my brother's girlfriend for clothes to wear. I dressed like a little old woman, wearing big tracksuits and jumpers that were ten times my size. Looking back now, I understand what I was subconsciously doing. I kind of blamed myself for being raped. I was drunk, so it must have been my fault. By dressing in those baggy outfits, I was trying to be ugly and dirty, because that's how I felt. That night changed me forever. I became bitter and was angry with my brother for not protecting me, even though he'd told our dad that he would look after me. The night after, I asked my brother if I could sleep in his room with him and his girlfriend. He said yes, so I dragged the mattress in their room. That's where I slept until my dad started paying for my rent at the Lionel Rose hostel. There, I had my own room, and food cooked by the staff. One of Dad's cousins and her kids had a room at the hostel during that time as well, and some nights I would sleep in their room with them. It felt good being around a family.

I started drinking alcohol heavily after that night. I'd drink anything that would make me forget about it for a little while. Most nights it was moselle, fruity lexia. Not only was this nicer in taste than beer but it was also a whole lot cheaper. But no matter how drunk I got each night, the next morning my problems would still be there. I got a job during this time in a takeaway food shop on the main highway. In my raggedy clothes, I wasn't presentable enough to work the front counter, so the boss made me peel potatoes and do odd jobs in the back of the shop. I didn't mind though, until he asked to see me in his office. I thought he had a more sinister plan for me, so I ran out of the shop and never went back, not even for my final wages. To say I had a mistrust of males is an understatement. This mistrust and insecurity affected me pretty much my whole adult life. Especially with relationships. It wasn't until I met my soulmate years later that these feelings would diminish. But I will tell you about that later, much later.

This is when I realised that I was wasting my money and time drinking. I rang my dad and asked if I could come back home to live with them, and promised that I would go back to school. So, I caught the train back to Melbourne, and Dad met me at the station. He had a job at the Department of Education and had just moved to Moonee Ponds with my stepmother. She and I get on really well and have a special bond. She has been like a mother to me, and I credit her for my love of books and reading — she is an avid reader and had a bookcase full of books that I would read in my room. My little brother lived there, too. It was the first time that he had lived with Dad for a long time. The house was really nice, with three large bedrooms and a bungalow in the backyard. We even had a veggie patch. The street we lived in was full of kids and laughter. My brother and I were in high school, which was only a short bus ride up the road. I was in Year 10 and my brother was in Year 8.

Brunswick High School was multicultural, with a lot of ethnic students attending. There were Greeks, Italians, Serbians, and Turkish kids. I'm pretty sure my brother and I were the only Aboriginal children there. It didn't take me long to withdraw myself from this school and find another. I found it hard to get along with people as I was quite rebellious. So, I shopped around until I found another school a few suburbs away, close to the city: Kensington Community High School. It was like the school from *Fame*. It was a dilapidated building, full of asbestos. From the outside, it looked like an old factory. I was going there for a while and then I enrolled my little brother, because I'd noticed that he was wagging a fair bit at the other school. We had done a semester before I told my dad that we'd moved. He just shook his head and asked some questions about the school. I thought that he would be angry, but he wasn't. He ended up being president of the P&T committee and saved the school from being closed down. He even got funding so that it could relocate.

At this time, Dad's sister — Aunty Dot — was missing, along with a man she was in a relationship with. The family had heard bad things about him, including that he was a woman-basher and a drunk. We hoped that she was okay, wherever she was. She was missing for years. We were all fretting for her. When I found out that she had left, it was as if my mother had abandoned me all over again.

Then one day, out of the blue, I heard that she was back in town, so I got on the next available train for the trip to Morwell. All I'd been told was that she was back, but not her exact location. I was determined to find her. I had enough clothes for a week packed, and I wasn't leaving until I found her. I knew I'd have to pretty much scour every known Aboriginal household looking for her. I had money from my weekend work at the local fruit and veggie shop, so I ordered a taxi, and off I went.

I considered going to my grandparents' house, but something

told me that if I had only just found out that she was in town, then they didn't know yet. So, as I reached the first of many houses, I yelled out from the front seat of the taxi, 'Is Aunty Dot here?' I did this a number of times, while keeping one eye on the taxi fare.

The second-last house on my search was one I knew very well. It was all lit up: no curtains, music blaring — the old faithful country and western — and as the taxi pulled up, I could see empty cans and bottles of beer strewn all over the yard, and the garbage bins overflowing with rubbish. I knew that if I yelled out nobody would be able to hear me, so I had to get out of the taxi, walk down the sloping driveway, and then up some stairs to the side of the house, where the front door was. The front door was shut, but I could smell the foul stench of alcohol. I banged on the door as hard as I could; I think my heart was pounding even harder though. I was getting worried. I was nearing the end of what I could afford with the taxi fare, and it was getting dark.

Suddenly, the front door opened to what was, I suppose, a lounge room, but there was no furniture. I could see a small girl. I asked her if Aunty Dot was there, and she replied, 'Yes.' I ran back down the stairs, up the steep driveway to the taxi, paid him, and got my bag out. I returned to the house. The front door was still wide open. I walked inside with trepidation.

I could hear voices coming from the kitchen, so I walked towards there, but the little girl must have told Aunty Dot that someone was there for her, because as I was nearing the entrance, my aunty appeared. We embraced and cried. I can't describe the emotion I felt at that moment. She looked different, as she stood there clutching a can of beer. I had never seen her drink alcohol before. It was a weird feeling. We didn't really catch up or rather, I didn't find out where she had been, because, before we knew it, other people were around us, and it was getting really loud. Shortly after, my aunty, between staggers, made me a bed on a single mattress on the lounge-room floor, next to a double mattress for her and her man. I plonked myself on the mattress, under the sheets, and went to sleep.

The following morning, I got up early. Everybody was still sleeping as I quietly left the house. I leant down and kissed my aunty on the cheek, whispered that I was in town for a few days and would see her soon.

After that, it was pretty much a blur. I went and stayed at friends' houses. Two days went by, and I was strolling down the main street of the town when a local Aboriginal I knew asked me if I had heard what had happened last night. I said I hadn't. They went on to tell me that Aunty Dot, her man, and a whole lot of other people were drinking around a brick barbeque area, often frequented by mob. Towards the end of the night, Aunty Dot's man started yelling at her, and then grabbed her by her hair and smashed her head and face against the brick, rendering her unconscious. This man had bashed her to within an inch of her life.

I ran as fast as I could to my grandparents, but they weren't home, so I assumed that they had already found out. I contacted my father and heard that Aunty Dot had been transported to a hospital in Melbourne for specialist treatment, including full facial reconstruction. During treatment for injuries sustained, my aunty found out that she was pregnant, and that most of her bones in her face were smashed beyond repair. The plastic surgeon had to insert metal plates in her face. It took months and months for her to heal properly. Behind the scars and the disfigurement, I can still see my aunty in her eyes. She is the most beautiful black woman I have ever met.

I returned to Melbourne, to some form of normality. I wanted to be closer to my aunty and to go back to school. The school was full of misfits; the students that attended Kensington had all been expelled from their previous schools for violence or drugs, and nearly all of them lived at the high-rise housing-commission flats. These kids came from broken homes, and were subjected to a lot of violence. Many of their parents were on heroin. I loved that school. I joined the school band and travelled around Victoria doing gigs.

There was a bit of a baby boom in our family over the next year. It seemed like everybody I knew was having a baby. My stepmother, my sister, my brother's girlfriend, my dad's sister, and, a year later, my mother. When my stepmother was pregnant, I was hoping that it would be a baby boy. I didn't want her to have a girl — *I* was Daddy's girl.

I wasn't home much during these days. I would sneak out my bedroom window and go hang out with my friends. One night, I ended up in Fitzroy with a friend. We walked past a pub that was notorious for drug dealing. As we passed the bar door, an older Aboriginal man walked out and gave me a black garbage bag, saying, 'Here, sis, you can have this.' I didn't know what was in there, but I grabbed it anyway. It felt heavy. I took it around the corner under the streetlight and opened it, and to my surprise, it was full of weed. I wasn't even smoking at the time. I caught a tram, train, and bus home with this garbage bag full of an illegal substance.

When I got home, I didn't want to go through the front door, as per a normal person, so I jumped in my bedroom window. Pacing the floor, I was thinking about what to do with this stuff. While I was pacing, I rolled myself a joint. Midway through the joint, it came to me. I rang my brothers and sister and told them what I had. The first word I heard was 'bullshit'. After much convincing, they couldn't get over to my place quick enough. I just gave it to them and wished them luck. The following night, I toddled off to the old Russell Street police station, where I was singing with the police choir. We were rehearsing Christmas carols for the upcoming Carols by Candlelight at the Sidney Myer Music Bowl. That was my first and last rehearsal, though, as I soon lost interest.

CHAPTER 10

By now, my little brother had dropped out and run away from home. He was hanging around our cousins in country Victoria, riding motorbikes all day and stealing cars at night. One night, the day before Valentine's Day, my brother and my cousin rang to say that they were on their way to Melbourne, and that I should wait up for them. Hours passed and they didn't arrive, so I went to sleep. I was awoken by Dad opening my door, crying, saying that my brother and my cousin had been in a car accident, and that my cousin was dead. He told me to just get dressed because we were leaving straight away. We had to drive two hours to where my brother was in the hospital. Halfway there, my dad was crying so much that the car was swerving. I don't think he could see the road through his tears. He pulled over to get some composure. I told him to get out and let me drive. I had no learner's licence or anything. He got out, though, and I drove the rest of the way. I stumbled through the gears of the car, we arrived in town, and I found my way to the hospital, where I parked the car and turned the engine off. We got out and ran towards the hospital entrance, where we spoke to a staff member and asked where my brother was. Directions were given, and then we were with my brother. Dad spoke to the treating doctor, who advised that he was injury free, and that he could be released immediately.

We walked my little brother to the car; he was walking slowly. We placed him in the backseat of the car and drove to my aunty's and uncle's house, the parents of the cousin who had just died. When we got to the house, we went inside. We walked up the cold, dark hallway until we reached the lounge room. The house was quiet. Family were sniffling and crying silently; you could feel the sadness in the air. The hospital staff had released my brother with just a hospital gown on, and he had no clothes. Dad told me to give my brother my baggy shorts and shirt — which were twice my size — to wear. I was handed clothes by my aunty to wear — my dead cousin's clothes. This did not sit comfortably with me.

Then we drove to our grandparents, who were staying at Aunty Dot's house. A bed was made for my brother in the lounge, and we all sat around. He was sleeping, and he looked really pale. Something didn't seem right. All of a sudden, he was violently vomiting. My grandmother said to call an ambulance; she thought he had internal bleeding and concussion. My dad called the ambulance, and he was taken to hospital. Sure enough — exactly what my grandmother had diagnosed. He was rushed into emergency surgery. Hours passed, with the whole family sitting in the waiting room. He made it through the operation and was put in an intensive-care ward. It was hard to see my little brother lying there, all busted up. He was lucky to be alive.

Back at the house, the family were planning the funeral for my cousin. He was just 17 years old, and due to turn 18 the following month. My brother was only 14. We spent a lot of time travelling between the hospital and the family home. When we got to the hospital on one occasion, my brother had finally awoken after his operation. The first thing he asked was if our cousin was okay and where he was. The doctor had advised us that we shouldn't tell him about the death of our cousin, as it could put him into shock, which wouldn't help his condition. The day before the funeral, my grandmother decided he needed to know. I can't remember who actually told him but I remember vividly his reaction. He howled uncontrollably. The following day, we collected him from the hospital in a wheelchair. He wasn't able to walk unaided and could barely talk. As he was wheeled into the church, you could feel everybody staring at him. Dad wheeled him to the open coffin where my cousin lay. He looked so peaceful, as if he were asleep. Draped around the coffin was his footy jumper. My brother stood up, kissed him, and then fainted.

After the funeral, my brother came back to Melbourne. He was different, quieter; he would sit in the corner and rock back and forth, crying. I would sit with him for hours and just let him talk. The boys had been drunk, and my cousin had stolen a three-tonne truck from a fully fenced wasteland site, driving it through a locked gate, causing an almighty bang as the gate flew open on impact. My brother had got into the passenger seat, and they'd driven to the next town, where they dumped the truck. They were walking the streets when our cousin spotted a car parked in the driveway of a house next to the Presbyterian church; presumably, it belonged to the pastor. My cousin hot-wired the ignition, and off they went. My brother thought they were going to our grandparents' house, because that's where our cousin and his girlfriend were living. They had a baby boy together already, and she was pregnant with their daughter.

My cousin was driving and was doing speeds of up to 180 kilometres an hour. My brother was in the front passenger seat when my cousin lost control and drove into a tree on the opposite side of the road. As the car was veering off the road, my brother saw the headlights of another car and thought that they were going to hit it head on; then he saw the tree and, in that moment, thought that he was going to die. He braced himself as he put his head between his legs. As my brother was thrown, on impact, out of the windscreen of the stolen car, he landed over a barbed-wire fence in a paddock. The impact must have been immense, because he'd been wearing his seatbelt. He lay there, unconscious, and only came to when he heard voices in the distance. He heard a voice closer to him, 'There's another one here.' He kept passing in and out of consciousness. The next time he could remember, he was in hospital.

My cousin died instantly, still seated in the driver's seat. My brother blames himself for our cousin dying, because just a second before the accident, he'd passed him a lit cigarette, and my cousin took his eyes off the road to grab it. You know the saying that when you're scared or frightened, you 'shit yourself'. Well, when my brother was thrown out of the vehicle, he *did* shit himself. This is why he had no clothes.

When my brother was released from hospital, the police interviewed him. They wanted to charge him with manslaughter for the death of our cousin, but they never could. My brother was the passenger, not the driver. If our cousin hadn't died on impact, still seated in the driver's seat, the police would have charged my brother with manslaughter. My cousin was pinned behind the steering wheel, and they had to use the jaws of life to free his body. When the matter went to court, the magistrate placed my brother on a two-year probationary period, and said that he had been through enough.

It took years for my brother to get over this. I don't think he is over it, really; he has just learnt to live with it. No one in the family has ever celebrated Valentine's Day again.

Recently, I heard that my aunty — the mother of my cousin — went to a clairvoyant, who claim she'd spoken to my cousin and wanted to tell his mother to pass on a message to my brother: 'Sorry', and 'I died quick, and I saw you standing beside the car looking at me.' Whether I believe in clairvoyants and fortune tellers or not, I'd like to think that she did actually speak to my cousin.

Since this incident, I've had a close bond with my little brother, and have tried to protect him. Even when he asked to borrow my car, some years later, and ended up in a police pursuit, smashing my car up and leaving me with no vehicle. After this adventure, I received a phone call in the wee hours of the morning, asking me to come to pick him up in a country town an hour away. What he'd somehow forgotten was that he had my vehicle — how was I to get there? I ended up borrowing a friend's car. I had strict instructions from my brother that when I got to town, I was to park in front of the town's post office, leave the car going, and have the back door unlocked with a blanket on the seat. I felt like I was a bloody character in a Bond movie, but I stuck to the given instructions. As I pulled into the parking space at the front of the post office, with no other vehicles in sight, all of a sudden, I saw a figure come running down a tree at the front of the post office. He opened the rear door and dived on the floor, covering himself with the blanket. He started screaming at me to drive. He stayed under the blanket pretty much the whole trip home. I think he even fell asleep. When we got back to my house, he told me that he got into a chase with the police, and was driving erratically through parklands, up and down gutters, until he did a runner. The police never caught him, which explains why he was waiting up the tree. I've never had insurance for that vehicle, and I had to pay a lot of money to have it repaired.

After this — and many similar incidents— I came to realise that although I can try and protect my little brother from other people and influences, I can't protect him from himself. There have been many times my brother and other family members have displayed self-destructive behaviour, especially under the influence of alcohol.

When I returned to school after the funeral, a lot of my friends had dropped out. I would still see them hanging around Kensington, totally wasted. They, too, had succumbed to heroin. I was no saint, but I never did hard drugs — I just smoked the odd joint.

I used to forge my dad's signature, though, on cheques in his name, and then cash them at the local bank. Technically, the money was for me, as they were Abstudy payments. My dad was never home in time before the banks closed. So really, I was doing him a favour. Dad would leave his car at home and take public transport to work in the city. Well, I used to borrow his car and drive around, often returning only moments before Dad would get home. He was none the wiser, because I would mark where to park the front tyres.

A few of my friends overdosed around this time. A sad waste of life, they had so much going for them — they just needed someone to care. I think that was the difference between me and them. I may have had a dysfunctional life, but I was always loved and cared about by my father.

CHAPTER 11

In 1988, I completed Year 12. I was one of only seven Aboriginals in Victoria to do so — I know this, because there was a camp for us, and I got to meet the other Year 12 Koori students. By the time I graduated, I was a bit of a loner. I didn't mind my own company, though. I had joined an Aboriginal band that played cover songs as a back-up singer: The Eagles, Credence Clearwater Revival, and some '60s music. I had a good repertoire of music and listened to the golden oldies every Saturday night on the radio in my bedroom. Sometimes I think I should have been born in another era — I love '60s music and Motown.

We did gigs at local pubs in Melbourne that gathered large crowds of the Aboriginal community. I figured out early that doing gigs was not going to pay the bills; I would leave at the end of the night with just enough money for a packet of smokes and a kebab. My dad was always at these gigs, which suited me, because I would scab a lift home in the taxi with him.

I had no idea of what career to pursue. I applied for university and was surprised to get in to study for a Bachelor of Arts. I was majoring in sports and English. I wanted to be a physical education teacher. I was also taking drama and music. My acting skills must have impressed someone, because I received a request from Universal Studios to audition for a role. Nope, not Hollywood — a small role in an even smaller production of the local playhouse theatre. I never tried out for this role.

During my short stint at university, my sister got a housing-commission unit in Broadmeadows. She was living there with her son, who was about 18 months old now. My sister had rung up my dad and told him she was having trouble living on her own; next thing, my dad packed up my belongings and told me that I was moving in with her. I had no say in it, and, more to the point, how was I going to get to university? It was a long way from her stinking little suburb, which I named 'the Bronx'. I bought myself a ten-speed bike so that I could maintain my fitness levels, and, more importantly, so that I had transportation to university. I was getting a small amount of Abstudy, but I handed all my money over to my sister for board and food. We always seemed to run out of food, but she never ran out of her pot. *Hmmm.*

One weekend, I decided I needed a break from eveything: her yelling all the time, and me caring for her son, and the time she ran a hot bath for him in the morning because he had shit all over him, and then, while the bath was running, she went back to sleep. My nephew woke me up, crying, standing in the lounge room in ankle-deep steaming-hot water. The water had been running for so long that it had leaked to the unit below us and caused damage to their furniture. When I came back from my break, my bike was missing. I asked my sister where it was, but she wouldn't answer me. When I looked out the window, I saw a strange woman riding my bike around the complex, and she was also wearing my bike helmet. She wasn't strange but a stranger to me. I found out some days later that my sister had traded my bike with this lady for a bag of weed. That was the final straw.

I packed up and went back to Dad's, whether he liked it not. If I learnt anything from my forcible stay at my sister's house, it was the art of fraud. She would get the phone connected, ring everybody she knew, but when the bill came, it never got paid and the phone would be disconnected. A week later, she would have the phone on again, in another name. Then there were the food vouchers. Yeah, we needed food, but she would get hundreds of dollars of food vouchers, and sometimes cash from different charities. They would even pay our electricity bill. My sister was very resourceful.

I continued to go to uni after I went back to Dad's, but I soon became withdrawn and lonely. I had no friends and found it difficult. In my first year, I was only 17 years old. When I did find my actual lecture rooms, I was always the youngest student. I had the habit of entering rooms and only midway through the lecture realising that I was sitting in the wrong one. Must say, I took down heaps of notes, though.

Gradually, I started to miss days and would pretty much sleep all day. I eventually deferred my studies; I didn't want to tell my father, as he had been so proud when I got in. I was the first person in the family to complete Year 12, as well as the first to attend uni. If I told him that I was no longer going, I felt I'd be letting him down. After a few months of pretending to go, though, I'd had enough. I told him — you should have seen his face. A face of disappointment, to say the least. He told me that I wasn't going to sleep in all day and that I had to get a job. I told him that the following day, I'd be approaching all the Aboriginal organisations in Melbourne for work. He must have notified the managers of these organisations to let them know I was heading their way, because the first one I attended, lo and behold, I got a job as the receptionist on the spot. My dad was well known and respected in the community, and I truly believe he had a lot to do with me getting the job.

This job was at the Aboriginal Legal Service. I moved to a better-paying position at another Aboriginal organisation after that. I worked out quickly that it's not what you know in the Aboriginal community, it's who you know. Every job I applied for, I got. I worked at every Aboriginal organisation in Melbourne: even an Aboriginal childcare centre called Yappera in Argyle Street, Fitzroy, which was my favourite. I started out as the cook, preparing and cooking nutritional meals for the babies and toddlers, then I ended up in the office doing bookkeeping. It was in the office that misbehaved toddlers were placed for a short period, before being allowed to go and play with the other children. My baby brother was attending Yappera during those days, and he purposely got himself into trouble so that he could sit in the office with me. I never kept any job for too long; I was young and naïve, and most of the time I felt bored. I felt that it wasn't stimulating enough, and I couldn't see myself doing that work my whole life.

We moved house to the inner-city suburb of Fitzroy North, which was closer to my work. It took fewer than ten minutes to get there by public transport. Sometimes while I was waiting for the tram, I'd start to walk between tram stops, and would be at work before the tram showed up. I was staying away from home more and more; I'd made a new circle of friends and would often stay with them at their house. It was a party house, and all we'd do was drink. Ouzo-and-cola UDLs were my preference, but I'd drink anything when they ran out. The house was always full of people.

One of my best mates at the time was an excellent football player, so we'd go watch him play every weekend; he'd get player of the match, week in, week out. I soon realised that the other people there — including my best mate — were doing more than just drinking grog, they were taking speed. I've always been dead against heavy drugs, so I planned on never trying it, but apparently one of the girls there was spiking my drinks. One night, we all went out to a pub in Fitzroy and my dad was there. He must have noticed that I was high as a kite on something. He walked straight up to me, slapped me hard to the face, and took me home in a taxi. I went back to the party house because I was missing my mates. A few days later, we were awoken early by banging on the door. It was the police — unbeknown to me, I'd been staying in a squat — and everyone was evicted. No time to get our belongings.

A few weeks later, there was a football carnival in Shepparton, and my best mate was playing in the local team up there. While on the footy field, he suffered a fatal heart attack. Died instantly. The post-mortem revealed that he had a high amount of speed in him, and his heart couldn't take it. I couldn't bring myself to go to his funeral. I have not seen any of my fellow squatters since.

I was doing a lot of things at this time, and not really caring about the consequences. After being evicted, I went home to normality, and an earbashing from my father. I caught a taxi home, which was a fair distance. Problem was, I had no money on me. I sat in the front seat, making light conversation with the old man driving, as we pulled into my street. I told the driver that I had to go inside to get the money. When I got inside, no one was home. *I should just run out the back door until he goes. Shit, I can't — he knows where I live.* I went into my dad's bedroom and started scrounging around. I knew he left coins lying around, especially 50-cent pieces. Then I saw a money tin — my baby brother's. He was too young to know what money was, so I figured he wouldn't miss it. I couldn't open it, so I went outside, tin in hand, and gave it to the taxi driver. The whole tin. I told him there was enough for my fare. He drove off. Later that afternoon, there was a knock on the door; my dad answered it and guess who it was? Yep, the bloody taxi driver. He'd kindly returned the tin — mind you, he'd emptied it. How nice of him. I never heard the end of it — my dad still brings up the taxi story to this day.

I was still drinking ouzo-and-cola every Friday night. I gave my dad money out of my pay, knowing full well that he'd give it back if I needed it. I wasn't yet of legal age to buy alcohol, but the bottle shop at the hotel at the end of the street sold it to me every Friday night. I'd sit in the gutter of their carpark, behind some parked cars, listening to the live music coming from within the hotel. They'd sell me grog but wouldn't allow me in the hotel. I didn't mind. After I drank my six-pack, I'd stagger home, which was just over the road. I'd throw my empties in the next-door neighbour's wheelie bin and then go inside.

Nearly every morning, I'd wake up and my baby brother would be nestled up in bed with me, the little brat. A cute brat, though. He and I are so close. I bought him his first bicycle for his first birthday. I searched high and low for that bicycle. It was bright blue, with cute little training wheels. I bought it in the city and travelled on the tram back home with it. Peak-hour traffic, too, I might add.

I turned 18 and went out pub-hopping with some friends. One of whom was a seven-foot-tall gay man. He was the coolest. I never knew he was gay until someone told me some ten years later. I was shocked — not shocked about him being gay, of course, but the fact that I hadn't known. We ended up in a bar where there was a reggae band playing. It was the best night. By this time, I was an old hand at pubs. If there was a pub I hadn't been to, then it wasn't worth going to.

During one of these pub nights, I hooked up with my dad's best friend's son. He was about four years older than me, and we had unprotected sex on many occasions. Unsurprisingly, I soon fell pregnant. I had been feeling crook for a couple of weeks, feeling nauseous, but still eating for the whole of Melbourne. So much so that my dad noticed my new eating habit and went and bought some worming tablets, and then told me to take them. I took the prescribed amount and vomited it straight up.

The next day, during my lunchbreak at work, I went to a doctor's clinic a couple of doors up. When I gave the doctors my symptoms, they asked me to provide a urine sample for a pregnancy test. *Positive.* I cried like it was the end of the world. I knew I had to tell my father, and that he would be pissed off with me. That afternoon, I told my boyfriend that I was having a baby. He was happy with the news and agreed to come with me to tell my father. That night, we told Dad. I was shaking. Well, his face went really pale. You know it's bad when a black man turns white. I thought he was going to kill me. He just said that he was disappointed in me and that my boyfriend had better look after me. A few nights later, I packed my clothes and moved in with my boyfriend.

I never drank alcohol after that; I even quit the band and stopped going out. It wasn't about me anymore; I had a little life growing inside me.

I didn't really know my boyfriend well, but what better time to get to know someone than while you're having their baby. We got on well enough and were getting excited about having a baby. We started picking names, and we agreed on a boy's name and a girl's name. With my pay, I started buying baby clothes. Neutral colours: lime-green, white, and yellow. When I had my first ultrasound, I didn't want to know the sex of the baby. I wanted it to be a surprise. The bigger I got, the more I loved this little baby inside me.

Our relationship didn't work out, so I moved back in with my father and stepmother until I gave birth. My stomach was massive, and I was due any day. I went to bed and woke up with the mattress all wet. I thought that I'd peed the bed. I got out of bed, still dripping, and waddled to my dad's and stepmother's bedroom. I woke Dad up and said, 'I've pissed the bed.' He said, 'Don't panic, daughter, but you're having your baby.'

CHAPTER 12

I was dropped off at the maternity hospital by my oldest brother, who happened to be staying with us. There I lay in the labour room, in the most pain that I have ever felt. The nurses told me that once I had the baby, there'd be no more pain. Almost 17 hours later — and after a herd of family coming in and out of the labour room — I gave birth to a beautiful baby. A healthy baby with light-blonde hair and green eyes. I cried when I saw my baby for the first time. When the nurse put the baby on my breast to feed, the baby took to it straight away; it was amazing. But I can tell you there was no dignity in that room that day.

The baby's father was there with tears of joy; he told the nurse the name. My baby was bathed by their father, and then he gave the baby to my father to bathe as well. My father would go on to bathe all my children when they were first born. He was there for me during all my labours.

When my baby was about three months old, I moved to Geelong and enrolled myself in Deakin University. Hail, rain, or shine, I was determined to do something with my life. I got a nice two-bedroom unit; it was very homely. I was given furniture by the course coordinator at my new university. I was going really well, taking my baby and breastfeeding in my lectures. Handing in my assignments on time and passing all my subjects. I got dropped off one afternoon by the uni bus. As we were approaching my unit, I saw a scruffy woman with yellow hair. You know the colour when someone has tried to dye their hair with household bleach and it's gone wrong? Then I saw a little boy from behind — he looked about five years old and was wearing really baggy clothes. I don't even think that the clothes this little boy was wearing would have fit me, and I'd just had a baby. These two were peering in my lounge-room window. I asked if I could help them. When they turned around, they were no strangers — it was my sister and her son.

I let them in and bathed my nephew. Poor little boy. My sister looked like crap. She had lost a lot of weight. I hadn't seen her for about twelve months, and she'd clearly been through a rough time. She had been living in Adelaide with a man we suspected was bashing her, but she always denied that to my dad. My little brother and I even drove to Adelaide once to plan her escape from this crazy man, but she wouldn't leave him. She'd finally had enough, though, and had left him and found me.

The stories she told me of the violence and abuse she was subjected to throughout her relationship with this man were horrific. The reason she'd always returned to him was that he would hunt her down and find her, which he did on this occasion as well. The first night she stayed at my place, he was on the roof, trying to smash my windows, until I called the police. I hid in the wardrobe with my baby and my nephew. I didn't want them around that. Some years later, he would kill his new girlfriend; he was charged and convicted of murder, and is now serving a life sentence in South Australia.

When my brothers found out that she had returned to Victoria, and that her crazy ex-boyfriend was terrorising us, they made their way to where we were. So, there we were — all four of us united again. We had funny nights, full of laughter, but they were so distracting while I was trying to study. My oldest brother came into a bit of money from criminal compensation. He had been stabbed by two complete strangers years before, whitefullas. He'd almost died and had required the length of his stomach stapled. When he was released from hospital, he'd stayed with Dad, my stepmother, and me. I had cared for him as he lay bedridden. So, to reward me, when he was given a pittance for his troubles, he took me to a used car yard and said, 'Pick a car.' I chose a maroon Nissan Pulsar hatchback, five-speed manual with a sunroof. I didn't have a driver's licence, but I had a car. I drove around everywhere — I even got pulled over by the police a few times, but only for a breathalyser. They never asked to check my licence. The one I never had.

One weekend, I drove to the country to stay with friends. It was here I met a guy who was Yorta Yorta, but living on Gunai/Kurnai Country, and we hit it off immediately. We got on well enough; he was funny, and my firstborn liked him. He was a childcare worker at the time, and so I thought he must be a good person. With a bit of prompting from him, we began a relationship. I left uni and moved in with him. I didn't know that I was making a mistake that would haunt me for years.

I began a relationship with him in 1991 and was soon pregnant. I remember vividly the first time he punched me. I was heavily pregnant, and he had left, taking all the money we had, and stayed away for three days. When he came back, he was with four of his friends. I asked where he had been. While I asked this, I was holding my older child on my hip. He walked up to me and, with a closed fist, punched me in an upward motion to my nose. I don't recall what happened after that, but I woke up, with my child, on the ground. My nose was bloody and sore. He was in the kitchen with his friends. I picked myself up from the floor along with my child, cleaned my face, and went into the bedroom.

I was abused and assaulted on a regular basis. Many times, I escaped and moved to Melbourne, and each time, he found out where I was. He would break into the house and grab my children, leaving me no choice but to get into his vehicle with him, or he would grab me by my hair and drag me outside. During these car rides back to Morwell, he would drive erratically, threatening to kill us all. He always threatened that if I ever left, he would kill me, and I believed it.

While seven months pregnant with my third child, there was a time he was driving, and I was in the front passenger seat. My other two children were in their car seats in the back. He started throwing punches to my head as he was driving, threatening to give me a proper flogging when he stopped the vehicle. I was so afraid that I threw myself out of the moving car. I ran as fast as I could to all the houses in the street. One house had its front door unlocked. I ran into the house, slamming and locking the front door behind me. An older lady came from another room as I ran to her telephone to call the police. He must have seen me running into that house, as he began banging on the door. The older lady was so frightened, and I was terrified. The police never came, so the older lady drove me to the doctor after he left.

When my youngest daughter was born, I decided to leave him for good, and got a two-bedroom flat in Morwell. He found out where I lived and would often knock on my front door. When I opened it and saw that it was him, I would try to close the door, but he overpowered me each time. He would enter the flat, punch me to the back of the head, go through all the rooms and then leave. This happened so often that I had a permanent egg at the back of my head.

From the flat I moved into a house in Mary Street, Morwell. He moved into this house, too. Not long after he moved in, one Friday afternoon, he bashed me in the bathroom while I was holding my four-month-old baby daughter; my oldest child was in the bathroom as well. I fell to the floor holding the baby, and covered her as he kicked my head and body with his steel-capped work boots. While he was punching and kicking, he was holding my two-year-old son, saying 'This is how you treat a slut, my son.' He dragged me into the bedroom and told me not to come out or he would flog me more. I could only leave the room when I needed to go to the toilet and each time, he dragged me back to the room.

As I sat in the bedroom, I heard him pulling the phone cord out of the connection on the wall. I knew this sound, as he often did this to stop me from calling police when he had flogged me. I stayed in the room with my baby daughter all weekend — I can't remember if I ate.

Monday morning came, and he was meant to go to work, but I heard him plugging the phone back in and telephoning his boss, saying that he was sick. I was praying that he *would* go to work, as it would have given me the opportunity to call police and to flee.

After this phone call, though, I didn't hear the sound of him disconnecting the phone again, and it soon rang. It was my brother's girlfriend, calling from Moe, asking if she and my brother could come stay at my house for a while. I said, 'Yes', and then he snatched the phone from me and pulled it out from the wall. I was dragged back into the bedroom.

About 30 minutes later there was a knock on the front door; I ran out from my bedroom and answered it, and my brother and sister-in-law were standing there. When my brother came inside, my abuser exited via a side door. My brother and sister-in-law were shocked to see me with two black eyes and covered in bruises.

After he left, I stayed in the house until my bruising went away, which took about a week. The next pension day I needed to go shopping. My car was broken down, so I decided to walk with my three children. The baby was in the pram. As I was walking, I saw him walking towards me, still at a distance, so I started running as fast as I could with the kids to an office block. I ran into an office, shut the door, and grabbed the phone to call 000. He chased me in and hung up the phone, then knocked me to the ground and bashed me in front of my children, the manager, and other staff. Nobody helped me or called police for me.

I was 23 years old, with three children, in an abusive relationship. I was evicted from every house I moved into because every payday, he would steal all my money and leave for days, only returning when he had run out. He wouldn't come home empty-handed though; he always had a bag of weed to keep him going until next payday. My dad bailed me out so many times during these days. He would send money for rent, food, and my electricity bills. I felt like a complete failure as a person, and more so as a mother. I had promised my babies that I would protect them, but I wasn't protecting them.

It was during this time that I found out that my grandmother had terminal cancer. She told my dad, and he told me, but I had to promise not to tell anyone else. She didn't want to be treated any differently. She and Grandad had moved back to Bung Yarnda, back in the Gorrie homestead, some three hours away, but they would often come and stay with me. They absolutely adored my kids. That would be the only time he would be on his best behaviour.

I couldn't believe that my life had turned out like this. Each time I reported him to the police, or they were called to our house by neighbours, I was told that they couldn't do anything. That or they would tell him to leave. They even took my babies from me and gave them to him, because by the time police came, I was the hysterical one and he was the calm one. I was at my wits' end.

When you are getting beaten, it does something to you. It takes away your self-esteem, your confidence, your self-respect, and your self-worth. But more importantly, it takes away your voice. I never told anyone I was being abused, not even my family. On the occasions I had facial bruising, I wouldn't leave the house until they healed. There were many opportunities I could have told my father and left, but fear takes over. The fear that he would find me. My father came most weekends with my little brother, who was three or four years old then. Dad would turn up unannounced and just pull into the driveway. Before they even got out of the car, he always told me that if I mucked up or if I told Dad, he would kill him and rape my little brother.

The only things I had to live for were my babies. Everything I did was for them — but I mainly needed to protect them from flailing arms and fists. Even when I was getting beaten up, I would be constantly thinking about where my babies were, because most times that's when he would strike me — when

I had a baby in my arms. He almost always attacked me from behind, so I never saw it coming.

While my brother and sister-in-law were staying with me, I felt safe, but I was still trying to think of ways to get out of town without him knowing. About a month later, late at night, there was a knock on the front door. I knew who it was — I must have sensed evil. My brother opened the front door and it was him, asking to speak to me. My brother shut the door and came and told me. I said no — I had a bad feeling about this. I always thought of the times he threatened to kill me. My brother said, 'Just go out there, I'll be watching from the window. He won't hurt you.'

I went out and was leaning against my brother's car when, without a word, he grabbed me hard by my throat, one hand choking me and the other punching me to my face. I couldn't breathe, I was trying to call out to my brother. I thought, *this is it, he is going to kill me.* My brother came running out of the house and knocked him to the ground. When he fell on his back, he still had a hold of my throat, so I was on top of him, still struggling for breath. My brother got me off and bashed the shit out of him. The police were called.

The next day, police came back and photographed my injuries. My whole face was swollen, with bruising all over. I couldn't even open my lips or eyes. My brother and sister-in-law looked after my kids until I recovered, giving me drinks through a straw because I couldn't open my mouth. I truly believe that he was trying to kill me that night, and if my brother wasn't there, then I would definitely be dead today.

CHAPTER 13

A while after I recovered, I met the brother of my new sister-in-law — they are both Gooreng Gooreng. We started a relationship. I didn't think it would last long, as I was damaged goods with three children. It did last a while, though, and I ended up moving to Queensland, to where he was from: Bundaberg. This was my escape out of hell. As we planned our trip, the only people that knew were my family. I caught the very first train out of town to Melbourne. It was still dark when I left. My heart was pounding as I boarded the train; I was waiting to get caught. I got to Melbourne and was met by my dad — he'd packed a hamper of food, drinks, and goodies for me and the kids. My youngest was only six months old, and I was still breastfeeding her. We were catching a bus to Brisbane, and when it arrived, we boarded and found our seats. When I looked out the window, I saw my dad crying while he was waving us goodbye. He made me cry, too, but I think my tears were happy ones, because I knew we were on our way to a better life, away from violence.

It was a long bus ride, especially with three little kids, but we made it. My new boyfriend was already in Brisbane and was waiting at the bus terminal for us. From there, we drove four hours north, to Bundaberg. I met his family for the first time. His parents were so welcoming and just loved my children. This man was not violent towards me; he never swore at me, and he was so loving towards the kids. The only time he raised his voice, I instinctively grabbed my children and ran and hid in a wardrobe. We sat there for the longest time — I was waiting for him to come and bash me, but he never came. I never did tell him what I did; he was probably wondering where we'd all gone. The kids began calling him 'Dad'. They truly believed that he was their father. I explained the truth to them some years later.

Bundaberg had a high unemployment rate, especially if you weren't educated. My new boyfriend had left school after Year 8. So, the only work he could get was picking tomatoes. Back-breaking work for next-to-nothing pay. I felt bad for him, because I'd got a job as the coordinator for an after-school program, as well as being a teacher's aide. When I went for the job interview at the school, I was actually applying for an assistant position, but the interview went so well, and they were so impressed with my resume, that they offered me the coordinator's position.

We were living in a poorly designed three-bedroom Aboriginal house. It only had one door, but we were paying cheap rent, so it didn't matter. The house was situated right next to a cane-field. One Saturday, while I was home with my children and their stepfather was at work, I was making lunch and went to the laundry to place the dirty tea towel in the washing machine. When I looked down, I saw a brown snake slithering through the screen door and into the house. I had always had an emergency exit plan with my children, and we had to use it then. We all ran into my bedroom, where I pushed the window screen out, and I pretty much threw my oldest child out the window — not a big drop, I must add. Then I passed my baby daughter out the window for them to hold and then my son. Then I jumped out the window, but realised I'd left my packet of cigarettes in the kitchen, so I climbed back in the window and ran up the hallway, past the snake, and grabbed my smokes. Back out the window again to my children. Mind you, when I sprinted back up the hallway, the bloody snake hadn't even moved. I had exercised this emergency exit plan like we were being physically chased. Long story short, the snake was removed by a snake handler; I had to pay an expensive fee only to learn the snake wasn't venomous, and the handler released it back to the wild in the cane field right next door to our house, where it had come from in the first place, and, no doubt, where it would come from again.

Before we moved into the Aboriginal house, we were renting a large Queenslander home by the Burnett river. About a month earlier, my little brother and my sister-in-law had also moved to Queensland. When my brother came over, he would always bring his guitar for a jam. Apparently — unbeknown to me and everybody I knew — there was a break-and-enter at a music store on the main street of Bundaberg. How has this got anything to do with me, you might ask? Well, a lot, as it happens. There must have been a police officer living in the same street as us who saw my brother with a guitar. It must be a crime for an Aboriginal man to own a guitar! One morning, it was still dark when there was a knock on the door. Just as I was getting out of bed to open the door, it was busted down, and ten large figures were running in the house, announcing 'Police! Search warrant!' Once I sorted out my early-morning blurred vision, an officer was explaining the warrant to me: he told me about the music store, and that they believed the stolen guitars were in my house. They searched high and low, all while my children were still asleep in their beds.

They came up with nothing — what a waste of bloody time.

The police explained that they had received information about 'people entering my house with guitars'. It was one person with one guitar. I felt victimised, and I told them so. I knew it was because we were Aboriginal. I was upset about the raid and wrote a letter to the media and the officer in charge of the police station, demanding an apology. The following day, the newspaper's photographer came to our house and took a photo of us. I had to tell my children not to smile. We ended up on the front bloody page of the local newspaper. I got my apology from the police, too.

Shortly after this, I got news that my grandmother was now gravely ill and that I needed to return to Victoria. I didn't want to go back to Victoria on my own, so I took my oldest child. I had a bad feeling about taking the other two children; I was afraid that their father would kidnap them.

A couple of days later, my oldest child and I arrived in Bairnsdale, Victoria, at the local hospital, to say my final goodbyes to my grandmother. It was enormously upsetting, seeing her lying motionless in her hospital bed. Unable to move because of a high dosage of morphine to help ease her pain. I sat beside her as other family members were walking in and out. We would all take turns sitting beside her. It was one of the saddest moments in my life, seeing how sad my father was. Knowing full well that my grandmother could go at any moment, and we would never see her again. A few weeks before this, I had been listening to a popular radio station, and they were advertising a Father's Day competition. All you had to do was send in a letter and tell them why your father should be father of the year. I'd put pen to paper and sent it off to the radio station. I wasn't sure what the prizes were, and nor did I care — I'd just wanted to tell someone how much my father meant to me. Lo and behold, I had won. The prize was music DVDs and CDs of all genres. There were heaps. Anyway, when I went down south for my grandmother, I carted this big box of music with me. It sure did cheer my dad up, especially the congratulatory letter from the radio station.

There was a moment when it was just my grandfather and me, sitting in the hospital room with my dying grandmother. I was on one side, holding her hand, and my grandfather was on the other. I started crying, trying to be really quiet. My grandmother opened her eyes and looked at me and said, 'Don't cry, daughter, I need you to be strong for your father and grandfather.' I wiped my tears, and I did not cry when her heart stopped beating and she was pronounced dead later that same afternoon. We lost the matriarch of the family that day. I kept my grandmother's wishes and remained strong until I returned to Queensland, where I sobbed.

I couldn't attend my grandmother's funeral, because a day before she died, while I was at my sister's house in the same town, there had been a knock on the front door. It was a solicitor, serving me Family Court paperwork and a court date. The father of my two youngest kids was taking me to court for full custody of them. Soon after this solicitor left, I received a phone call from him, saying that if he saw me at my grandmother's funeral, he would put me in her grave with her. I took this threat seriously, and soon after my grandmother's passing, I got permission from my father and grandfather to leave the state. I found out later how he had managed to track me down: apparently, his older sister had won Division 1 in TattsLotto, and had hired a private investigator to find me.

I not only returned with my oldest but also with my sister's son, who was eight years old at the time. She asked if I could look after him for a while, as she was going through some troubled times. I would have this boy on and off for the next ten years, more on than off. I never received any government benefits for him, and nor did I want them. It wasn't about money; I wanted to give this little boy a good life and a happy childhood.

A day or so after arriving back in Queensland, I made some phone calls and contacted a solicitor to represent me in the Family Court. There would be lengthy phone calls, planning for the big day. My solicitor got permission to represent me without me being present, due to the threats my ex had made and the previous violence. I was so relieved hearing this, but not so when I found out that the kids' father had won access for school holidays and two weeks during the Christmas break. It was November, and the next access would be Christmas. This meant that I had to travel to Brisbane and hand my children over to their father. Not only was I fearing for my safety when I did this, but I was so worried that I would never see my children again, because I knew what their father was capable of. Prior to handing my kids over, I was strictly advised by my solicitor to stick to the court order, as hard as it would be — if I didn't, then the courts would give their father full custody, and me access. And if he didn't stick to the order, then he would lose access. This is the only reason I handed my children over — because I knew he wouldn't adhere to the order.

Two weeks later, my children were not returned to me as stipulated. I made calls to the Victorian police and my solicitor, and the matter was passed on to the federal police. The feds located the kids eight weeks later with their father, at a random address. They handed my kids over to my father, who drove them back up to me. I was frantic the whole time they were away from me. My son was only three years old, and my baby daughter was just 14 months old. My solicitor took the matter back to the Family Court, and their father was charged by federal police for kidnapping, and lost all visitation rights.

It has been more than 20 years since then, and my children have still not seen or heard from their biological father, except for when he attempted to contact them via social media, asking to meet them. My son, who is now a fine young man, politely responded, 'Due to the unspeakable wrongs you have done to our mother, we do not want to know you.' Although my children know all that I went through, I have never discouraged them from meeting their father. I have always left this decision to them.

CHAPTER 14

A few months after this, I married my then boyfriend, having a traditional wedding reception with proper bush tucker — dugong and turtle. All my children, including my nephew, were in the wedding party. My father walked me down the aisle and was crying more than me. My grandfather was also there; he had been hospitalised with pneumonia the day before, but he wouldn't stay in hospital because he wanted to see me get married. We would be married for eight years, but we separated and divorced when my ex-husband left me for another woman. That wedding was one of only two times in my life to date that all my family came together.

After marrying, we decided to move to western Queensland, to Biloela, so that my husband could get a better job at the meatworks. I wasn't worried about finding employment; I was pretty confident that something would come up. When we arrived, we settled into the local caravan park for the night. I didn't want to stay there long, so the following day I went house-hunting and found an affordable home. We stayed in this house until we were offered a large house from Aboriginal housing. This house had been newly renovated and had three large bedrooms, and a granny flat with two more bedrooms and a toilet. The yard was massive as well, with a mango tree full of fruit. My husband started work immediately at the meatworks, and the kids were enrolled in their new school. I even started the kids up in Little Athletics. They had fun, and we did a lot of travelling with them to compete. My son played rugby league, which also required him to travel to different towns, but I arranged for him to get lifts with other team mates for the away games. It had been about six months since the move, and I was still unemployed. I approached the only aged-care home in the town and offered to do voluntary work there until I could get a paying job somewhere else. They gladly took me in.

I had the best times at the aged-care home. Getting to talk to and read mail to the old people. I got to feed them and call out the bingo numbers for the weekly bingo session. The prize was chocolates. One afternoon a week, I brought my kids in. The residents enjoyed seeing my children. There was an old Aboriginal resident in the facility, and the whole time I was there, not one family member or visitor came in to see him, so I would take my kids into his room. He thought we were his family. I never had the heart to tell him otherwise. He died a couple of years later, which was sad, because it felt like I lost a family member.

One day, reading the local paper, I saw that there was a job vacant at the high school for an Aboriginal teacher's aide in the special-needs department. I approached the Aboriginal elders of the town and asked if I could apply for this job — I didn't want to move to a new town and take the locals' jobs from them. I was given permission, so I applied and was successful. Sadly, due to the demanding hours at the school, I had to stop at the old people's home. I made a lot of friends through working at the school, though. I started an Aboriginal basketball team named Murri Magic, and coached them. There was only one good player on the team — and not only was she good, she was the only one who knew the rules of the game. It was fun playing other teams — which were coached by the PE teacher — during lunchbreaks every Friday.

My nephew had gone back to his mother for a bit, and, in the meantime, my aunty sent her 14-year-old son to me, as she was having troubles with him. I told her that I would sort him out, but explained that if he played up for me, I'd send him straight back to her. When he arrived, I bought him a new bed and bedding, a school uniform, and books. I discovered that he had been learning to play the trumpet at his old school, so I arranged for him to borrow a trumpet from the school and he joined the school band. The only Aboriginal kid in it. Then I entered him in the army cadets. He was given a full army uniform and boots. I was so proud of him, and he just loved it. Especially when he went bush with the other cadets. He was a good kid, well-mannered, and my kids loved him and treated him like a big brother.

During these days, my husband was smoking marijuana, and, more shockingly, he had started dealing it. We argued about this — I didn't want it in my life or my kids'. He continued to make promises that he'd stop. One afternoon, I found out that my little cousin had been caught smoking my husband's marijuana. I put my cousin on the next plane back to his mother, and I kicked my husband out of the house, and told him he could return when he gave up smoking and selling marijuana. He was gone for about three weeks, with a promise that if I got into the police, then he would give it up for good.

This came about because while we were living in western Queensland, I'd been reading an Aboriginal newspaper, *Koori*

Mail, and had seen an advertisement about joining the police force. I thought I would give this a go. When I applied, I had to complete extensive applications and send them to Queensland Police Service Headquarters. Once that application was approved, I was invited to attend an interview. I was so nervous but I dressed to impress. If the interview went well, they'd ask you to do the fitness test, which was held the following day at the police academy. The fitness test was a 2.4-kilometre timed run. I ran like I was being chased and just made it in the specified time. After this, I had to attend a government doctor for a medical test, which I passed. Then I went back home and waited to find out whether I had been accepted into the police. When I told my dad, he came up from Victoria to await the news with me.

While I was waiting, I was doing my own training: running laps of the school oval and doing push-ups, all the while listening to Vanessa Amorosi through my headphones. Finally, the letter arrived. I was accepted and given four weeks to start. This meant uprooting my family and moving to Brisbane so that I could attend the academy. Just weeks before the news, my oldest child won an academic scholarship to travel to New Caledonia for a student exchange. They never got to go, due to us leaving, and they still go on about missing it.

I immediately started browsing the newspapers for any accommodation close to the police academy. There were only a few houses for rent, so I rang all the numbers provided. I was eventually offered a lease on a house, and, with research, I found out that the house was in the next suburb from the police academy, and there was a school for the kids close by. The house was in Darra, on an estate full of old army-barracks homes from the 1960s. My husband got a job at the meatworks in Dinmore. Everything pretty much fell into place. The primary school my children were enrolled in was predominantly Vietnamese students, which I thought was wonderful for my kids to be around: to be able to learn another culture and for them to share theirs.

About two months later, my little brother, my sister-in-law, and their children moved to the big smoke. They stayed with us until they found their own home. It was good having family close by, and cousins for my kids to play with, as I waited for the next stage of my life to begin.

PART TWO

BLUE

CHAPTER 15

I joined the police for several reasons: first, to see if I could get in, and more importantly, because I had seen the way police mistreated my people and naively thought that if I joined, I would be able to stop this. I thought that by being in the police, I could help to eliminate or eradicate the fear and mistrust my people have towards police. After only a short time in the force, though, I realised that those fears were well and truly justified.

I wanted to help people in the community, people of all backgrounds — the needy, the vulnerable — and to treat them with respect and dignity. I wanted to treat victims of crimes and family-violence sufferers with the compassion and understanding they deserved, and to take their complaints seriously. Unfortunately, it wasn't that simple. Police as an institution in Australia is mainly white, dominated by men, and built on systemic racism, misogyny, homophobia, and bullying. Police target not only my people but also other minority people in the community, which explains the higher recidivism rate these communities often display.

Police recruit black and brown people as part of their

'Cultural Capability Action Plan', but I — and other Aboriginal police before and after me — know that this is tokenistic. Instead of addressing the overwhelming representation of my people in the justice system and prisons, police want to be seen to be doing their bit for reconciliation. So they employ more black people, which isn't the answer — no amount of black cops can make things better if the force itself is still racist.

During the time I spent in the police I witnessed police brutality, excessive use of force, black deaths in custody, and ongoing racism. This was soul-destroying, and I lost ten years of my life that I can never get back.

When I applied for policing, I applied through an Aboriginal traineeship program. This course involved twelve months at a TAFE, completing a justice course, as well as spending Fridays at the academy, so that the trainees would become familiar with being there. Once you passed that first year, you were accepted into the Queensland police academy as a recruit. When applying, we sat the same entry exams as everyone else, but the training took longer.

On the day of the assessments, there were about 40 of us at the police headquarters. We were called into a large room, where we were to take the psychometric assessment, which would take anywhere up to four hours. I took my seat, as did everybody else, and silence fell in the room as a sergeant explained to us the procedure. When the sergeant stopped speaking, I picked up my lead pencil and began the assessment. It took me about three hours. When I put my pencil down, the sergeant approached me and said I could leave the room and get some lunch, and to be back in an hour for the results.

I walked out of the room and followed the short corridor to the main entrance of the police headquarters. As soon as the doors slid open, I felt the heat of the day hit me in the face, and the sound of traffic and people rushing about their day brought me back to reality. I had been in a trance-like state for the last three hours, hoping but not sure if I'd passed. I walked around the city aimlessly for a bit then found a café, where I ordered a coffee, and waited until I saw some people who'd been in the same room walking back towards headquarters. I sculled the remainder of the coffee and followed them, fast.

We sat in the hallway, waiting. Then, all of a sudden, a door was flung open, and I heard people's names called out. My name wasn't called out, and my heart sank. I watched as everyone whose names had been announced walked into the room. They were only in there for about five minutes before the door was flung open again, and they all walked out. The sergeant then called out the remaining names and told us to come inside the room. There were only five of us left. Four males and me. We took our seats, and I heard the sergeant say, 'Congratulations; you have passed the assessment.' Those words were the beginning of my police career.

One of the guys selected for the Aboriginal traineeship completed his Diploma of Justice, and attended the academy every Friday with us, but failed the final fitness test. The remaining four of us felt gutted, as we'd spent so much time together and got to know each other so well. I still have contact with one of them who, like me, was later to be subjected to racism and trauma. He and I got on well at the academy. We were in the same squad and sat next to each other and hung out together every day. I don't think I would have been able to stay at the academy without him, or remained in policing as long as I did — he was the person I called whenever I was subjected to racism. He is my little brother for life.

Training to become a police officer was rewarding but

difficult. Seven months of intense learning about a variety of legislations; exams every two weeks, with a pass rate of 65 per cent. The physical training was full on, which I thoroughly enjoyed. In my intake, there were four squads, made up of 25 people of all ages. We came from different walks of life, but all had the same desired outcome of becoming a police officer. That was pretty much the only thing we had in common.

I got on well with everyone in my squad. I would cram for exams the night before and was getting marks of 75 per cent. Then there was the driving and firearms training. I loved driver-training the most — driving fast and pursuit training. I aced all the requirements on the first go, while others had to have two or three attempts before they passed. For firearms training, we had an exam, which I got 100 per cent on, but when it came to the actual firing of the Glock, I passed all requirements except for the night shoot, and had to repeat that part. To be honest, I think I have bad eyesight — poor night vision, at least — but I didn't tell anyone. They would have failed me or made me get tests for my eyesight and put me into another squad. If it turned out my vision was very poor, I might have been asked to leave the academy. This was the same with any injuries incurred during training; you'd be put back in another squad to give you time to heal. But no one ever wanted this: you wanted to march out with your own squad, because you were a tight group and good mates. So, unless it was broken, you kept on going.

The first two weeks of attending the academy, I had to wear civilian corporate attire. Then they would load us on the academy bus to take us to the police warehouse, where we were to be fitted by a tailor for our uniforms. But on this particular day, just before boarding the bus, I felt a bit peckish and decided to run to the canteen at the academy to buy some fried dim sims, which I devoured in seconds. As I was eating, my bloody front tooth broke in half. You have no idea how shamed I was. I couldn't go on the bus like everyone else; I had to report to the academy doctor, who sent me to a dentist to have the tooth repaired. It wasn't until the following day that I attended the police warehouse, which was deadly because the only other Aboriginal person in the squad was *also* absent the day our squad went to get fitted, so we went together the next day. I had never been to a single place in my life that I left with so much clothing, and so many shoes and other items, other than a second-hand shop. It felt like a shopping spree. I was given sets of uniform— shirts, pants, police overalls, jumper, boots, Doc Marten's shoes, blue woollen police socks — plus a police traffic vest and a utility belt, which my gun holster was attached to. I was also given handcuffs and a retractable police baton. I felt awesome, and I couldn't wait to get home to show my family, because I knew that they would be just as happy.

Every morning, all recruits would have 'parade', where we would march in unison to be inspected by senior officers. It was very regimented, similar to the army. At the academy, they even taught us how to iron our uniforms and where all our creases should be. When the senior officers inspected, they were checking for our creases. There were consequences if we weren't dressed to their standard. I didn't mind the drills and the dress code. We were different in looks, but we were dressed the same, right down to the creases.

When I was going through training, I was a smoker. The smoking area was called 'Jurassic Park'. It was surrounded by large overgrown bushes in the centre of the academy. At any given time, before and between classes, there would be up to 20 of us smokers, including an Aboriginal guy who had completed the justice course at the same TAFE as me. So, I'd known him for a year and a bit before I saw him again at the academy. He was living at the academy, in the dormitories, and drove a gold-coloured Ford ute. One morning, all the smokers piled into Jurassic Park, but I couldn't see him. I joined a chattering group as I puffed on my cigarette, and I realised they were talking about the guy. The night before, he'd been driving around looking for a ute similar to his — but not just similar, he wanted one of the exact same colour. He drove and drove, and then he couldn't believe his luck — he found one in an industrial estate. It was parked outside a business; it was late, and nobody was around, so my mate had walked up to the ute and removed the metal petrol cap. He'd lost his and was using a plastic one. Then he drove back to the police academy and went to his room, preparing for the following day.

As he sat looking through legislations, there was a knock on his door. When he opened it, he was surprised to find a plain-clothed police officer there. The officer asked him to accompany him to the local police station, where he was led into an interview room. My mate was shocked and frightened; he didn't know what was going on. He was in there a few minutes when uniformed officers came in and set up the interview tapes for a recorded interview. Sitting there, stunned, he finally got up the courage to ask what was going on. An officer explained to him that the industrial estate where he'd stolen the petrol cap had been occupied at the time by a police officer conducting a covert operation, and his crime had been witnessed. My mate was interviewed, sacked, and told to leave the academy immediately. I haven't seen him since; I spoke to him some weeks after, but he was embarrassed to speak about it. I just wished him well. For months and months, he was the butt of a few jokes at the academy.

While I was at the academy, I didn't get to see my children as much as I needed to. So, every opportunity I had, I would bring them to the academy to play on the oval or swim in the pool with me. I wanted them to see where I was when I wasn't with them. I also did this so that they would feel comfortable around people in police uniform. I was trying to break the cycle of 'fear of police' for my children. I would tell the kids about people I'd met at the academy, and what sort of jobs they had before they joined, and if they, too, had kids and a family.

And then, finally, induction day. I marched in as a recruit and out as Constable of the Queensland Police Service. All my family were there: my mother, my father, and my children. Only two of my brothers weren't there. One couldn't come due to other commitments, and the other wouldn't come because he hated police with a passion. By now, he'd had a few run-ins with them and each time he was bashed, brutalised, and mistreated.

I got to witness his passion on a couple of occasions.

The first was after I had become a police officer. I was having a family barbeque at my house and invited my brother and his family. Throughout the afternoon, he was drinking alcohol and eventually became too drunk to drive, so I asked him to stay the night and made up beds for them all. As I was going to sleep, my sister-in-law started yelling out my name. I walked out of my bedroom and saw my brother punching into my fridge and then walking towards my brand-new coffee table. This coffee table was a piece of art. It had a three-inch glass top and was resting on a large dolphin. So, while he was trying to smash my house up, I gathered my children and placed them in my vehicle, and then I called the police. I never wanted my children to witness violence again. It was the middle of the night, and I told the kids, 'Lock the car door, and don't let anybody in except me.' I ran back inside my house and could see my brother was still behaving violently. While I was grabbing things, I could hear the muffled sounds of my kids screaming. I ran back to the car, where my brother was running around, punching every window of the vehicle, trying to smash them. I saw my kids' faces as they were screaming. They were so frightened. I had to do something and act quickly. All my training had to come into play right then. So, I grabbed my brother, put him in a choke hold, rendered him unconscious, and put him on the ground until the police arrived. As the police turned up, my brother was just coming to, and the young police officer handed me the handcuffs to cuff my brother.

It would be months before I spoke to my brother again. I always forgave my family when they played up, though. No sooner had I offered my brother forgiveness, then off we'd go again. This time, my sister-in-law and four of her children turned up at my house in the middle of the night, due to his alcohol-fuelled violence. We put her children safely in bed and then were sitting out in the lounge room so she could tell me what happened, when all of a sudden, in the distance, I could hear screeching tyres as they turned corners, as if a vehicle was travelling with speed. I knew it was my brother. I woke my oldest child up and told them that I was going outside, that they should lock the door after me and not open it other than for me. I also told them to call the police.

As I got to the front of my house, my brother's car pulled up, and he staggered from the driver's side, smelling of alcohol. He started yelling for his partner to get in the car. I told him to leave. He didn't like this, and started throwing punches at me, which I ducked. We were in the middle of the road by now. I kept him in the middle of the road, away from my house, until I could hear the sounds of the sirens. I told him police were coming but that never stopped him. He was still trying to throw punches. When the police arrived, it seemed as if every police vehicle in the district had turned up. Police are very protective of their own. My brother ran off to my backyard, and then to my back door, banging on it. He wanted to hide in my house, but my daughter wouldn't let him in. I saw police running after him until he was captured and handcuffed and placed in the back of a police vehicle. When I returned to work, I was so embarrassed, but I knew that I couldn't control the behaviour of my family. I gave my brother the silent treatment for months after this episode, but once again, I forgave him. I felt bad about calling the police, but I needed to protect my children.

But back to induction day. It was such a proud moment when I marched out of the academy — even more so when I was the only female out of 150 recruits to be given an award. After the ceremony, family and friends were given morning tea, while all constables were called back into the stadium. There, we were given our police badges; all that hard work seemed worth it. As I received mine, I felt eyes on me, so I looked towards the entry door, and there stood my father, looking proud as he wiped tears away from his eyes.

I couldn't wait to get home and to finally relax. I'd done it. I was a police officer. Other than when I gave birth to my three beautiful babies, this day was up there with the best days of my life. When I got home, there were presents for me from my family, and a huge cake with writing on it: 'Congratulations, Constable Gorrie.' What an awesome surprise after an exhausting day — or rather, after an exhausting seven months. I had two days of rest before I was to start my very first shift at my new police station. This police station was in what police considered to be one of the roughest areas, with a high rate of drugs and crime. I was so excited and could hardly sleep. During their first year, constables are rotated through all police stations and specialised areas in their police district; then, when the year is complete, they're given a 'permanent' police station, in which three years must be completed. After the three years, you could remain in general duties or apply to perform duties in a specialised area. As a first year constable, you are supervised. You spend the first two months with one police officer, who is senior to you and has been trained to train you. They are called field training officers. After that two-month period, a first year constable is able to perform duties with any officer. The first year constable is given a field-training book with competencies that must be completed and signed off by the field training officer. These competencies included items like traffic infringement notices, communication skills, and reports in relation to jobs that you attend. This book had to be signed off by every officer that you worked with during the 12 months.

CHAPTER 16

I'll always remember my first job as an officer. My partner and I were called to the local McDonald's after a complaint by the manager that a female was injecting drugs in one of the toilet cubicles. The academy doesn't train us for jobs like this; they just teach you theory. When we arrived, I entered the female toilets, and sure enough, there was a toilet door shut. I went into the adjoining stall, climbed up on the toilet, and poked my head over the cubicle wall. There I saw a female with syringe in hand, injecting a drug into her groin. I yelled out to her; she was shocked and immediately got off the toilet seat, and then I saw her place a clear plastic bag in between her legs and pull her jeans up. I had to kick down the door and restrain her. When we got back to the police station, my partner — also a female — placed her in a room for me to conduct a strip search. At the time I was thinking, *I don't get paid enough money for doing this*. I felt it was the ultimate act of invasive intrusion, and it was dehumanising — it was deprivation of a basic right, and in any other context, it would be seen as a sexual assault. I was never comfortable doing strip searches. As she stripped, I directed her to bend and squat — sure enough, a plastic bag with white powder inside was protruding from her nether regions. My first job: a drug user, a strip search, and then an arrest.

I rotated through all stations and specialised areas in the police district. I learnt so much more in my first month on the road then I had at the academy. Almost all of the jobs I attended I could relate to, because I'd experienced it in my own life. But I never told my partners. There were domestic violence cases by the dozen, assaults, pursuing stolen cars while items from the vehicle — including beer bottles — were tossed out the window at the windscreen of the police vehicle. There were a lot of hairy moments chasing stolen cars, especially when they drove at speeds over 150 kilometres per hour, and on the wrong side of the road. They didn't care; they just didn't want to get caught. Most times, we would have to call off the pursuit for safety reasons. On the rare occasion when we would apprehend the offenders in these stolen vehicles, I was shocked to find out that they were often only kids, 16 or younger. These kids should have been tucked neatly into their beds.

But the most heart-wrenching scenes were kids as young as 13 injecting heroin into their bony little arms. These would often be the same kids that were stealing cars, joyriding for something to do at four o'clock in the morning. Inexperienced, high on drugs, they were accidents waiting to happen, and many accidents did. There were several occasions when a carload of kids would get into a stolen car, drive at high speeds and crash, torn metal flying around, the stench of burning tyres. The car would be smashed beyond repair, and the joyriders would somehow get out of these wrecks and run in fear of being arrested, while their cousin or best friend would be trapped inside the vehicle, dead. Not one of those kids ever came back or stayed at the scene to check on their family or friend.

Although I understood though why they would take their chance to get away, rather than stay and risk being brutalised by police, it upset me every time. Car crashes involving fatalities and young people always reminded me of my brother and cousin's accident.

Police not only brutalise people with excessive force, but they are racist, too. If they weren't racist prior to joining the force, in my experience, it seemed that they quickly became so. They would learn to target black people. Police out patrolling or on their way to a job who saw a black person driving would intercept the vehicle, and it didn't matter what kind of black you were. I heard so much racist language used by police during my time in the force. Sudanese were called 'skinnies'; Samoans and Tongans were called 'Pac Islanders', and Aboriginals were called 'abo' or 'atsi'. They were often categorised in crime groups as well: Pacific Islanders as violent and unlicensed drivers; Sudanese as thieves; Vietnamese as drug dealers; and Aboriginals as all of the above. During foot chases involving black people, I've heard other police call out, 'Stop running, ya little black cunt!' Black this and black that.

I had a Tongan friend in the police, who was on light duties when she was pregnant. She was in the station one day, talking about what she might call her new baby. The duty sergeant called out, 'Defendant!', and the room erupted in laughter.

Since I left the force, police have been issued with body cams. It doesn't surprise me in the slightest when, after allegations are made about the conduct of police during an arrest, the footage from those body cams disappears.

When you make an arrest and the matter goes before a

magistrate, it is the responsibility of the arresting officer to complete a statement of the facts of the arrest and then to ensure all other police, corroborating and attending, provide statements as well, to form the brief of evidence. Back in my early career, these statements were printable. The arresting office would hand out his or her statement to all other officers involved. When you were handed a statement, you knew that yours would have to align with theirs, whether it was true or not. If you didn't align, you would be treated like shit, and talked about within the district. Nowadays they have a file-sharing system, so there's no need to print them. Officers don't just plagiarise statements; some are making money on the side by writing essays and assignments for other police who are undertaking studies to go up rank: constable-development programs and the sergeants' courses, for example. I know many officers who have done this.

I also know that during an arrest, police will interview suspects who are intoxicated or heavily influenced by a drug. These people could be incoherent, but police don't care as long as they get their admissions; and often, if they aren't high on drugs, they're hanging, and will say almost anything to speed the process up, so they can be released.

It's a running joke within the police that police are the biggest criminals. It's not unusual to hear the saying 'Trust me, I'm a police officer' met with laughter. It was common for personal items to go missing from desks. I had a plain-clothes holster stolen, and when I asked who took it, nobody answered. There are complaint mechanisms in place, but to my knowledge, no one ever complained.

I recall a few times, while working with male work partners who had recently split up with their wives or girlfriend, that we spent most of the shift conducting drive-bys of their former homes, and in some cases, the ex-partner's new home. This happened quite a lot in my first year, and I didn't feel comfortable saying anything; I didn't really have a voice. I even recall that one of these men — who was having a custody battle with his former wife — fabricated a family-violence report, naming himself as the aggrieved, the victim, to improve his chances of getting custody of the kids.

Years later, when watching TV, I was also reminded of the time a detective sergeant from the Criminal Investigation Branch (CIB) was keen on me, but I wasn't keen on him. A story came on the news about a high-profile murder in Brisbane, and the investigating/arresting officer from the Homicide Squad was being interviewed by the media. It was him.

The event I remembered had happened on my day off — it must have been a weekend, because the kids and I were swimming in the swimming pool of our unit complex. I got out of the water, wrapped myself in a towel, and was walking to our unit to get some cold drinks when I saw an unmarked police car at the front of the complex. When I looked towards the driver seat, I saw that it was him behind the wheel. He just stayed there, watching me. I pretended I never saw him. For him to know where I resided, he must have either followed me home or looked me up on the police computer. I never told anyone about this; I probably should have, though. I'm not sure if he did anything like that again, but I was so shocked by it that every time I had a job that involved CIB, I avoided him.

Back when I was a first year constable, there were a few of the old boys still loitering around the police station like asbestos. They were five or so years off retirement, so to justify their existence, the roster clerk would roster them to work with a first-year every so often. To say that they were useless is an understatement; it was like the blind leading the blind. They would tell stories of their heyday; so many funny stories about jobs they'd had and the things they'd got away with. Like the time one of the old boys was working in the watch house; he used to take a bottle of alcohol to work and have a few sips during his shifts — he was pretty much a chronic alcoholic. When other police would bring in a drink driver, and the driver played up and wouldn't blow into the bag, the ever-so-sober old dog would threaten that if they wouldn't blow, then he would.

One time I was rostered seven nights with an old dog who refused to let me drive, and, the same time every night, he would pull over on the freeway under an overpass to have a bloody sleep for an hour or two. I'd be sitting in the passenger seat of the police vehicle, listening to the police radio of all the jobs going. 'Code 2' this way and 'code 2' that way. I would even see other police vehicles racing to jobs with lights and sirens on passing us. And then there was another old dog who refused to wear a firearm whenever he was on the road — except for when he worked with me, because I reminded him that if anything happened to me as a result of him not being able to protect me, then he would have the responsibility of caring for my children until they completed university. Off he would go, up the hallway to the gun safe. I didn't mind working with them because I was always the lead officer at every job; not because they didn't want to do the jobs, but because they didn't know what they were doing due to the fact that they were stuck in the '80s and since then, laws had changed. But once a copper, always a copper.

Most days, though, I found it very daunting. Not only was I a female in a male-dominant work environment, but I was also an Aboriginal woman, and later a single mother. A minority. I felt like a fish out of water, like I didn't belong. The number of racial slurs about Aboriginal people and other minority groups in the community that I heard nearly every single shift — well, sometimes it was too much to bear. If I was paid a dollar each time, I wouldn't have to work for a living — I would be rich. There were even a few occasions I thought about quitting. I was getting tired of it, and senior officers as high as senior sergeants and inspectors were among the main offenders.

Finally, I'd had enough. I spoke up after the time I was asked by two senior officers *how* I was Aboriginal. I explained, only to be told that I'd probably never been to an Aboriginal mission. I told them about Bung Yarnda; I explained what a mission was. The most senior officer said that Bung Yarnda was probably full of shops and more like a town than a mission. They asked me how many bunties I had, and if they all had the same father. 'Bunty' in language means arsehole. I was so offended and upset by this. I didn't know what to do; I was only a first-year officer and I felt so isolated. I had nobody to speak to; the only thing I could think of doing was putting in a formal complaint. Complaints in the job are unheard of — when you do shit like that, you're considered a dog. The complaint never went anywhere — I just got an apology from the two officers. And they wonder why Aboriginal police officers have a high rate of quitting. When I first joined the police, I had this idea that I could change the attitude of the Aboriginal community towards police. Little did I know I couldn't do that until I changed the police attitude towards Aboriginal people.

On another occasion, I needed to transport a prisoner to a watch house outside my district. I telephoned prior to leaving to get the correct address. I was told, by the male sergeant that answered, that they were on 'Gin Street', as in, 'Aboriginal woman'. I was appalled; I got off the phone and told my boss that I didn't want to do the transport because I couldn't be responsible for my actions when I spoke to the sergeant upon my arrival. After calming down, I did the transport, and when I got there, I asked the male sergeant if he was the person I'd spoken to on the phone. When he said, 'Yes, who wants to know?', I replied, 'The Aboriginal woman that you were speaking to.' His jaw dropped.

One of the hardest aspects of the job was that whenever I was put in a car with a police officer that I hadn't worked with before, I would, within the first two minutes, somehow have to bring up the fact that I am Aboriginal. Otherwise, they could think that I was a whitefulla with a deadly tan. But more importantly, I didn't want to hear any racist remarks about Aboriginal people, my people, during the shift. On a few occasions, I *was* told that I had an excellent tan. I would tell these coppers that it wasn't a tan, it was my natural skin-colour, because I am a black person. I even heard a remark that because I was fairer, I was better than darker Aboriginal people. Racism lives and breathes in the police. As recruits at the academy, everyone is given cultural-awareness training about Aboriginal culture. I wondered where these people were on that day. It amazed me to think that these very same people, who held positions of such authority in the community, were racist.

When I first joined the police, I was partnered with a female officer who was to be my partner for the next eight weeks. She was my field training officer. It was evident from the beginning that she didn't like me. She didn't try to hide it; she had no patience for me and told me I should quit the job. One time, I was at the computer typing out a traffic accident report, and she was sitting about a metre away from me but behind me, in earshot. I could hear every word she was saying. She was sitting with other police officers, all men, talking about me, saying that she didn't know why I was in the job and that I should quit. I heard them all laughing. I printed out the report, and had to cut it to fit on a hard-copy proforma, which is what we did during that time — nowadays it's all on the computer. My scissors skills were not up to her standards, and she came over to me and said loudly, 'You can't even cut straight — what's wrong with you?' I was so upset and embarrassed that I walked into the boss's office and asked if I could be partnered with another officer.

From the moment I put the uniform on, I had to justify why I had joined. I was told three times in my first year that I should either quit policing or become an Aboriginal police liaison officer, due to my concerns about how police were treating my people. I was also told numerous times that, as a police officer, I was being a 'good role model' for my people. It never bloody ended.

After this, I was partnered with a male senior constable who was of Samoan descent. We hit it off immediately — perhaps because we were both minorities.

My new partner told me about some of the jobs that he'd had. The ones that had never left his memory. One in particular stood out, and he still had nightmares over it. He'd been working a morning shift when he was called to attend an abandoned-vehicle job. When he got there, he saw the car, but it wasn't abandoned as reported — it was occupied by a mother and three children. The mother, who was Aboriginal, had filled the car with carbon monoxide and poisoned the kids. All of them were deceased. There were twin girls aged about two years old, and a boy two years older. The girls had long, curly, sandy-blonde hair. The mother had tried to kill all of them, including herself, because the father of the children had committed suicide a month earlier, and she couldn't cope without him. It was just so sad.

As my new partner was talking, I saw tears in his eyes. He told me that he'd carried the bodies of the children out of the vehicle. He paused, then told me that the mother wanted to die as well, but he'd found her before she had passed. She was devastated. She was left alive while her three beautiful children perished. The mother was subsequently charged with the murders of her children, but it never went to court, as she was deemed mentally unfit. She was sentenced to a mental health facility but before this happened, she was allowed to attend the funerals of her children, who were all buried at a cemetery beside an Aboriginal elder.

You can spot an off-duty copper from a mile away. They're the ones sitting with their backs to the wall, scanning the room with their eyes. Forever on edge. Hypervigilant. Some say that you're only a copper when you're on duty. That's not true; you're a copper 24 hours a day, seven days a week. As hard as I tried to switch off while off-duty, it was extremely difficult. I lived in the same district that I was policing in, and I would spot offenders that we'd been chasing for months for outstanding warrants, or for other serious crimes. I couldn't just let them be — I would always call them in. These off-duty arrests earned me awards from my inspector for outstanding work.

One afternoon, while I was driving home from work, I was wearing my police uniform but had a large overshirt covering my police shirt. My children caught a train to and from school, and on their way home, they would get off the train and wait at a designated spot for me. They never waited long — maybe five minutes, maximum — but that probably seems a long time when you're an impatient teenager, which they all were by now. While they were waiting on this day, my oldest child was seated on a park bench when they heard a sound coming from across the road, as if someone was calling out for them. When they looked, they saw a white man standing on the verandah of the house, wanking in front of them. They got up from the park bench and walked away, but the wanker called out again, trying to get their attention. Unbeknown to me, I've pulled up, happy to see my children waiting for me. They all got in the car, and my oldest told me what had just happened. I got out of the car and told them to point the house out to me. While they were doing that, the wanker came to stand on the front verandah. I told the kids to get in the car. I gave my mobile phone to my oldest and said, 'Call my police station and get a crew here; tell them I'm gunna kill the wanker, so that they get here quicker.' I pointed my finger at the wanker and yelled, 'You, get over here now.' He came marching over at pace. I thought he was going to hit me, so I was ready for him. When he was directly in front of me, I said, 'I need you to wait here with me, I've got a police car coming to arrest you.' Sure enough, a police car soon came to a screeching halt, and he was arrested. He was charged with wilful exposure, and, because he'd exposed himself to a minor, he was placed on the sex offenders register. After this, my kids and I came up with another designated area for the pick-up.

Another time, I had finished my shift and driven home. My children and I were living in a gated block of flats at the time. Fenced and secure, or so I thought. On this night, as I approached the gates and entered the code on the keypad to open the gate, I saw a white van parked on the side of the road alongside the units. The occupants appeared to be acting in a suspicious manner. I thought that it was odd that they be there at that time of night. It would have been two o'clock in the morning — as I'd travelled home, I had been the only vehicle on the road.

My unit was towards the front gates. The gates opened, and I quickly drove my car in. I got out of the car, ran up the stairs to my unit, and looked out my bathroom window. One of only two windows facing the front of the unit. The other window belonged to my son's bedroom. I had to stand on the side of the bathtub to see out of this window. I stood there quietly, just waiting. I wasn't sure what I was waiting for, but I always trusted my instincts. Sure enough, I saw headlights, and then the white van drove past my unit. The van stopped, and I saw two people, a male and a female, get out of the van. I wasn't sure where they were going as they walked in the shadows of the unit blocks. I couldn't hear them — all I could hear was the sound of my own breathing. I held my mobile phone in my hand tightly, getting ready to call the police.

Then all of a sudden, they reappeared, pushing a motorbike into the van. The owner of the motorbike lived just two units up from me. I phoned my police station. When the duty sergeant answered the phone, I told him what was happening. He arranged for a crew to come and have a look. He kept me on the phone, which was just as well, because the van soon drove out of the unit blocks. I had the sergeant on the phone as I ran back downstairs and into my car and tried to locate the van. I lost them; my little car couldn't catch up to them. The whole time I was telling the sergeant the direction of travel. I eventually hung up the phone and went home to bed.

Over the years, I learnt to turn a blind eye — or, as we used to say in the police, put the blinkers on. I couldn't put the blinkers on when I went to my local petrol station and saw two men that were wanted on warrants, though. Police had been trying to capture these men for a long time. I had just worked my last shift and was going on a tropical holiday. I'd thought I would get into the spirit and was only wearing a sarong. I almost always carried my mobile phone, but as Murphy's Law would have it, I'd left it home on this occasion. I saw the two guys and ducked down in the car so that they couldn't see me. As they walked across the road towards Red Rooster, I got out of my car, walked into the petrol station, and asked the attendant if I could borrow their phone. I got an odd look from the young guy working behind the counter. I told him I was a police officer. An even stranger look — probably thinking, as I stood there in my bright sarong and a pair of flip-flops, *sure you are*. I rang the station and spoke to a constable, telling them about the men. The whole time, I didn't take my eye away from Red Rooster, staying on the phone until I saw police entering the carpark. I got back into my car, and soon enough, I saw police walking the two wanted guys out of Red Rooster in handcuffs. Apparently, they'd been found together in a toilet cubicle, shooting up heroin. I received a commendation from the superintendent for this off-duty arrest. That went on my personal police file and would come in handy when or if I applied for other positions.

CHAPTER 17

I spent 12 months in general policing, which required me to attend all sorts of jobs and take crime reports. These jobs ranged from break-and-enters to stealing, domestic violence, and assaults. Most of the jobs were trivial, except for the odd suicide or fatal traffic accident. I will always remember my first dead body. It was a very hot day, and my partner and I were called to attend. When we arrived, I saw a middle-aged male lying dead on the floor of his lounge room. Other police turned up and were looking around when one of them opened the fridge door and saw a slab of cold Coke cans. This copper grabbed a few of the cans and handed them out to his fellow officers. I didn't grab one, not because I didn't want to, but because I didn't drink Coke. When I was offered a can, I must have given an odd look, because the officer said, 'Well, *he* won't be needing them anymore.'

Police have a dark sense of humour. Morbid, too. They laugh at things that the general public would be shocked by. I think that's what used to keep me going. Whenever I had a dead body, I would always be immediately hungry, almost starving. After the job, I would go get a feed straight away. I think this was my way of desensitising. There are some smells and items that remind me of dead bodies now. For example, a Holden twin-cab ute — I once had two dead bodies from a speeding Holden twin-cab ute. This vehicle had only travelled 50 or so metres from a driveway before colliding into a power pole. The sound of the crashing vehicle alerted a resident who came out to investigate. When he walked out his front door, he saw two dead men on his front lawn. Due to the impact, both had been thrown from the vehicle.

While doing the graveyard shift — from ten at night until six in the morning — almost always, especially when you were really tired, two hours before your shift would end, you would get a 'dead-body job'; these notoriously took hours to complete. Quite a bit was involved in these jobs. You would have to arrange for CIB to ascertain the circumstances of death, either natural causes or other. 'Other' could range from suicides to homicides. General duties could establish this, but for protocol purposes, CIB had to attend. In some cases, we had to rummage through the pockets of the deceased to ascertain their identity. One time, I attended a scene where a man was mowing his yard and had attempted to move his trailer to another part of the yard. As he attempted this, he suffered a major heart attack, and collapsed and died. Well, it turns out that he was in the only shaded area of the yard. On this particular day, the temperature reached the mid-forties. So, until all services arrived, CIB and Scenes of Crime (SOC) unit, the deceased, and I all shared the only shaded area of the backyard. SOC attend scenes of crime, traffic accidents, almost all jobs including dead bodies to take photographs and fingerprints. In remote parts of the state, where these services were hundreds of kilometres away, the attending officers would take photographs of the scene. If it was deemed that fingerprints and other forensic materials should be gathered, then you would have to wait at that scene until they arrived, and that could be hours and hours. On this occasion, the neighbours handed me a fold-up chair over their side fence and a nice glass of cold water.

Then you'd have to arrange for SOC to attend to take photographs in situ, and then arrange for the government undertakers to attend and transport the deceased to the morgue. You had to attend the morgue and complete all the relevant paperwork for the coroner. While doing this paperwork on computer, the body would be less than a metre away from you. If your partner was doing the paperwork, the other officer would empty all pockets of the deceased and bag their valuables, jewellery, and money. In special circumstances, for cultural reasons, their clothes. Aboriginal people required the clothing that their loved ones passed away in.

On another graveyard shift I was with a junior officer, who had been in the police for about eight months. By now, I was a field training officer. We got a job to attend the local hospital as a female patient had died in the emergency department. This woman had travelled from Canada the day before to see her daughter and newborn granddaughter, and had begun suffering pain in her legs and feeling generally unwell. This woman was also Indigenous, so I knew that the daughter would be wanting her mother's clothing. I informed the nurse of this, but she didn't seem too keen to do it as she left the room, so I did — but not before the drama unfolded. As I was trying to remove the woman's clothing, I somehow managed to unhook the bloody catheter, which swung around in the air like a sprinkler. I was drenched in urine before I could grab the catheter and bend the end, like a hose, to stop the flow. The nurse, who already seemed to be cranky, yelled at me for making a mess. So, in front of junior staff, who was by now in stitches laughing, I had to rinse my police shirt with water in attempts to wash the piss off me. An absolute mess I made. So, whenever I would see that junior officer at other jobs, with other partners, it took me back to that scene, and we would look at each other and start laughing.

A correspondence (corro) shift usually means you stay in the office and do any outstanding paperwork required for court. Well, the police station I was working in at the time was opposite a row of shops: a supermarket, a butcher, and a newsagent, to name a few. The newsagent delivered newspapers to local residents. The delivery guy would drive the streets, throwing newspapers from the car window. One house he delivered to, he noticed that the resident hadn't grabbed their paper from the front yard for seven days. So he came to the front counter of the police station and reported this. The counter-shift officer rang the crew on the road, but they were tied up with another job, so he and I decided to go there and have a look. As we pulled up to the front of the house, I could see newspapers strewn all over the front yard, as the delivery guy had reported, and I also saw that on the inside of the house, the front windows were covered with flies. I immediately knew that this was not going to be good.

We knocked on the front door. No answer. The door was locked, so we walked around the house, looking in windows, calling out for the occupant as we did. Still no answer. When we got to the rear door, my partner turned the handle and the door opened. As we entered, several cats scattered, and a dog came out of a room, snarling and barking at us. It was a medium-sized dog, a labradoodle. A nice-looking pedigree dog with dry blood around its mouth. After clearing all the other rooms of the house, we entered the room the dog had come out of. An elderly female lay on the floor, lifeless, with one arm raised to the air. Only it didn't look like an arm, but bone. Flesh around the arm had gone. It turned out that the elderly female lived there alone and had lain deceased for days; with no one to feed the cats and dog, they ate the only thing they could — her. That explained the dry blood. I have never looked at a labradoodle the same way.

I never got used to the suicide jobs I attended. Young people hanging from trees; inside their wardrobes with a belt wrapped around their necks; lying in bed, hanging from the bedhead. At my new station, we had a young person from the local high school completing their work experience in the administration area. She was a lovely person, with the biggest smile. She went home one afternoon and had an argument with her boyfriend, who decided to end their relationship. Well, she ended her life after hearing this. Her mother found her hanging from her bedhead. It was so heartbreaking and senseless to me. The hurt that is left behind is unbearable.

Another that stands out to me is that of a man who was married to an Aboriginal woman, and had twin girls, with curly locks down to their shoulders. They were a young family, living in a nice suburb, but like all young couples do, they had their ups and downs. On this particular night, they were arguing, so the woman went to stay at her friend's home. She took the girls with her. The following morning, she went home, ready to speak to her husband. She searched the house for him, without luck, before going downstairs, where her husband spent a lot of time, as he had a bar and a pool table in his 'man cave'. She looked around but didn't see him. She called out his name but no answer. Then she looked towards a darkened corner and saw something. As she got closer, she saw it was her husband, hanging on the side of the garage rollerdoor. He was standing, leaning forward, with both hands clutching an extension cord wrapped tightly around his neck. At many suicides I attended, I would see similar sights — hands at whatever was around the neck as if they were trying to loosen it; as if they had changed their minds and wanted to live, but it was too late.

The wife called an ambulance and was hysterical during the call, saying that her husband was attempting suicide — she thought that he was still alive. When we got there, though, and upon inspection, it was clear that he had been deceased for some time. By now, the house was crawling with family and friends. I went upstairs and made cups of teas and coffee for the wife and the family. I also kept the twins occupied while my partner was speaking to their mother. I spoke to the best friend of the husband, who told me that the night before, the husband had been to his house and told him about the argument. He'd said, 'I'm going home to kill myself.' The friend took no notice of that comment, thinking that he wasn't serious. As I spoke to him, I could see regret all over his face.

My partner and I had left the house and the body had been collected when, over the radio, I heard another job for the same address. This job came through as a disturbance. The neighbours had called police to report a lot of 'Aboriginal people next door' who were being really loud, and wailing could be heard. Police communications was asking for any unit to attend. I immediately got on the radio, asking them to disregard that job. I explained that the disturbance the neighbours could hear was family members grieving for a death at the house overnight. I also explained that when we grieve, we can be loud. I spent so much of my time in the job educating people about my culture. It was so draining.

I hated nightshifts with a passion. One night, my entire role was to sit at a crime scene with another officer. One at the front of the house and one at the rear. As I was senior to the other officer, I chose to sit in the police vehicle at the front, as it was the middle of winter. The crime scene was a burnt-out house in which a male had been discovered, lying on a bed, after the fire had been extinguished. He hadn't died of fire-related injuries, but of a gunshot wound to the head. The perpetrator had burnt the house down to cover up the original crime. Cases like this are the reason that whenever police get deceased bodies, we have to check for suspicious circumstances. I had the heater on and fell asleep. I woke up to daylight, with an inspector knocking on the police car's window. The whole circus could have passed me that night, and I wouldn't have known. A few days later, a sawn-off shotgun was found by young boys in an industrial bin at their football club. I had to retrieve the firearm and drop it off to forensics.

As much as doing overtime on the graveyard shift — or on any other shift — is tiring, it also means more money. On one particular night, my partner told me he didn't want any overtime, because he had plans for the following day. So, of course, two hours before our shift was to end, we got a dead-body job. We attended the house initially for a welfare check. The wife of the deceased had called from interstate — she'd been trying to make contact with her husband without success. They were both in their early thirties, from another country, and had only just moved into the area. We knocked on the door and could see someone lying on a mattress on the floor. This person appeared non-responsive, so we had to force entry. When we entered the room, the familiar odour of death greeted us. We checked the body for any signs of injury but found none. A real mystery, this one. Young male, no history of illness, and no injury to suggest any foul play. This would definitely incur some overtime. My partner told me again that there was no way he was going to do overtime; he had somewhere he needed to be, come daylight. I wasn't fussed either way.

We called the district duty officer (DDO) on his mobile phone and told him our predicament. A DDO has the rank of senior sergeant, and they work every shift alone. They attend jobs where their approval is required by law. For example, it was the DDO's permission we needed to gain entry by any means — smashing a window, busting down the door — when we had someone non-responsive in a house, and needed to enter without the home owner's permission. This is the rank and position I was aspiring to. So, after the DDO called the next shift, and told them to take over from us, we did the only thing we could think of — we sat in the lounge room and watched television to kill time until they started. With ole mate lifeless in the bedroom, we sat in his lounge room watching telly.

Many times, jobs I attended as the arresting officer made the news. I would be doing my job, and then I would see television cameras filming. In saying that, there were so many that didn't. Like the young Aboriginal cop, who had only been in the job for about six months, who, on his day off, went into his police station in the adjoining district to mine, went into the gun safe, and loaded his firearm. He then drove an hour to the beach and shot himself in the head. It was devastating. Then there was the time an elderly lady drove her car into the river. Two teenage boys were standing on the jetty on the river, fishing, when all of a sudden, a car drove at fast speed down the boat ramp into the cold, murky waters. The young boys dived into the water and swam to the sinking car. When they tried to open the door to free the elderly lady, they found her door was locked, as were all the doors. They felt increasingly hopeless as the minutes went by. They finally surfaced and ran as fast as they could to a house for help. Apparently, the elderly lady had taken her own life. I felt so sorry for the young teenage boys witnessing this.

CHAPTER 18

So not only was I trying to get through my first years of policing, I had other, more important, issues to tend to: my family. At the end of every shift, I would say my goodbyes to everyone at the police station, and tell them I was going home to where my real job was — my children. They meant everything to me, and I was missing them so much. During my early years, I did a lot of crazy shifts, long hours, night work. Nightshifts ran from ten at night until six in the morning, but most of the time, I would get jobs that required overtime and wouldn't get home until midday. I would be so exhausted I'd just crash when I got home and wouldn't see my children for days. My husband and I broke up during this time, too.

I treated everybody I encountered while policing with respect and dignity. It didn't matter if they were drug addicts, offenders, or if they suffered from a mental illness. This came in handy: there were times when I would be wrestling around on the ground, trying to handcuff a violent offender, when all of a sudden one of my drug offenders, someone I'd arrested many times, would come up and ask if I needed help. I smoked cigarettes, which is a filthy habit, but this habit, too, came in handy several times during the course of my career. I would often hand out my cigarettes to calm people down, or I would buy them soft drinks.

This same respect wasn't always afforded to me by other police, though. I recall when I had been in the job for two years, a new policy was being rolled out. Random breath tests for alcohol were being given to cops, on the day it rolled out. Have a guess who was the first cop that had their breath tested for alcohol? Yep, me — not so random after all. Not only do police racially profile their arrests, it became evident that they also racially profile minority police officers — black cops.

On one occasion, we were called to the psychiatric hospital, where they had independent living quarters for some of the patients. The call was that a female resident had doused herself in petrol and was holding a lighter, threatening to ignite herself. By the time I arrived, there were about six officers attempting to calm her down. As I exited the police vehicle, I could hear her screaming in a fit of rage. As I got closer, I could see her, her arm extended, holding a red lighter. I said hello to her, and pulled a cigarette out of my packet, feeling around in my pockets for my lighter. I never pulled it out, though — I asked the female for a light instead, and she came towards me and handed me her red lighter. I walked away with it, and this gave the other officers present opportunity to apprehend her without incident.

Another time, I was at the end of my shift, and finishing off paperwork before I left the station to go home. A job came over the police radio about an Aboriginal man sitting on the roof of a house, refusing to come down. Not his roof, I must add. I knew this man; I'd had many dealings with him. I thought, *if I don't go there, police will be there all night*. I had visions of them trying to talk him off the roof for hours and hours.

I got in the police vehicle and drove to the house. As I pulled up, there he was, sitting up there on the roof looking really comfortable, smoking and flicking his used butts to the ground where other police were trying to talk him down. I walked into the middle of the front yard where he could see me, yelled out his name, and said, 'Get off the fucking roof — I need a light for my cigarette!' He said, 'Okay', and down he came. I told him off for scaring people and said next time he wanted to sit on the roof of a house, to sit on his own. Problem solved.

Then came news that my grandfather had been diagnosed with Alzheimer's and dementia. He was in another state, and the family didn't know what to do with him, as he required attention and refused to move into an aged-care facility. My oldest brother had by now moved to Brisbane to be closer to my little brother and me. So, the family moved my grandfather up to live with him, but my grandfather was stubborn and wouldn't listen to him. After every shift, I would have to go and check on my grandfather, making sure he would wash. The bathroom door had a gap at the bottom, so I would run the shower, strip Grandad to his underwear, and tell him to get in the shower. Then I'd go out of the bathroom and get on my hands and knees to look under the gap of the door, where I'd see my grandfather's black feet just standing there, outside of the shower, while the water was running. I took to standing in the bathroom with him, and putting him in the shower, and making sure he was soaping himself. It was getting stressful for my brother, so on my days off, my grandfather would come to my house. By now his dementia was really bad; he still knew who we were, but he had the classic case of the wanders. On several occasions, he just walked out of the front door of the house while my brother was sleeping or in the shower. We had to call the police to help us search for him. On one occasion, he was missing for hours before my brother plucked up the courage to tell me. I called the police and reported him missing, and gave them all the information they required: description, height, clothing, all the usual. I even gave them a recent photo of him and asked them to do a press release, as I had grave concerns for his safety and wellbeing. During the search, I received four phone calls from police officers also searching for him, asking if I thought that he was in a pub somewhere. I told them that he never drank alcohol and that he wouldn't be there. I was getting frustrated — I knew that they were only asking that because he was a black man — but I didn't have the energy to deal with that. Some five hours later, my grandfather was located, walking alongside a busy freeway that led to the western suburbs, wearing his thick rain-jacket. This would be normal, only it was a stinking-hot day.

Eventually, my grandfather went back to our other family in Victoria, where he was placed in a nursing home, as his health had deteriorated to the point that he could no longer speak. A few years later, I received the inevitable phone call from my father to come down, as my grandfather was close to death. It took me twelve hours to get to him in his hospital bed. He was still alive but non-responsive. I told my father and aunty to leave the room and go home, so that I could be with him on my own. I sat beside him and sang to him in his ear, his favourite songs. I thanked him for being such a good grandfather to me, and for being my best friend. I stood up, telling Grandad that I would be back soon — I was making myself a cup of coffee. As I walked out of the room, though, something made me walk straight back inside and sit next to him; it was as if I had walked into an invisible wall. I told him, 'I'm still here, I don't want a coffee now.' I wasn't sure if he could hear me or not. Then I knew it, because Grandad took a gasp; he took his last breath. I screamed the hospital down and rang my father to come back to the hospital. The nurse came and closed the door to the room. My father arrived with other family members and when they left, my cousins and I wheeled my grandfather to the morgue.

My father is an incredible man. He is my best friend. I look at him as if he is superhuman. He was always there for me when I was a kid, and more so as an adult. He has provided me with the safeness and the security that every child craves. There were many times when I was raising my children on my own, and struggling financially, that my father would drive two hours and buy me groceries. Then there were times when I needed hospital treatment, for dehydration and other medical reasons, and my father, without complaint, would travel to look after the children. One time, when my youngest was only three months old, I became really sick and needed to go to hospital, and he came down and cared for my babies, each time bringing food and goodies for the children. There has never been a time, when I've needed him, that he has let me down.

I recall one night when I was working a 2pm–10pm shift. My children were just reaching their teenage years, and my only son called me to say that his older sibling was having excruciating pains in their back and couldn't move, and that he had called the ambulance. I drove straight back to the police station, unloaded my firearm and put everything away, and then drove as fast as I could home. When I got home, my oldest child was crying, tears rolling down their face in agony. The ambulance soon arrived, and the paramedics administered something for the pain and then took off to hospital. I raced across the road to ask my neighbours if they could look after my youngest, and quickly explained what was happening. My son and I raced at breakneck speed to the hospital. Once in emergency, the nursing staff and doctors wheeled them to have an X-ray. After this, I was asked to go in a little room with the doctor where he told me that he thought my child had broken their back. I just broke down in tears. He was asking if there had been any sudden impact, like a car accident. I couldn't think of any way they could have broken it. After what seemed like an eternity, my child was discharged with a whole heap of painkillers, and with instructions to lay flat on their back on a hard surface until they saw a specialist. When I got home, I made a bed for them on the lounge-room floor, but because we felt sorry for them, the other two kids and I slept on the floor as well.

I telephoned my father crying, explaining the situation, and he asked me to let him know when the specialist appointment was. Sure enough, he travelled hundreds and hundreds of kilometres to be there. My father has been my rock in my life. Today I tell him that he is my best friend.

Over the years, I have tried to be there for him the way he has been for me. I spent many nights sitting in a chair beside him while he was in hospital being treated for a brain aneurysm. I recall one day I was working a dayshift and during it, my stepmother rang the police station asking to speak to me. I knew before she spoke that something was wrong with my father. By night's end, I had flown to be by his side. He had internal bleeding and required emergency surgery. He almost died.

I would often lend him my ear, listening to some of the harrowing jobs he had been involved in while he was employed in a senior position at the Department of Human Services. He once was heavily involved in a high-profile case where a little Aboriginal boy was reported missing by family, only for his body to be discovered under their house. This case went on for years, with police deeming it murder. To this day, despite police having their suspicions of who killed this little boy, nobody has been charged. This case destroyed my father. He would never be the same again, and he's still seeking psychological treatment. He has since retired, but not before receiving a Public Service Medal in 2005. He was the first Aboriginal man to receive this prestigious award. He deserved it, too.

Nowadays my father lives with my current partner and me. He suffers from dementia and has serious health problems, which makes for an interesting day. We still have big yarns, though. One story that has been etched into my memory is that back in the day on the mission, when he was growing up, police and welfare would barge into homes and check food cupboards. If they deemed them to be empty, they would remove the children. The old ladies cottoned on to this, so they started keeping all their old, used, and empty tins to put in the cupboards as a decoy. This behaviour remained with the old people for many years. My father told me that he once received a phone call from a grandmother who was caring for her grandchildren, and she was so frightened of the authorities coming and checking her food pantry, she was storing empty tins of food in her cupboard. All she asked my father was for him to let her know when they intended on going to her house — I guess so she could prepare her cupboard. After this, my father made it compulsory that welfare staff who attended addresses checking children not be allowed to look inside food cupboards or fridges, due to the stress and trauma it caused people.

CHAPTER 19

I got to know my usual drug offenders — the Aboriginal ones. I knew their families and the pain and hurt that they suffered as a result of addiction. In the community that I was policing, there were no community-based rehabilitation programs for Aboriginal drug users, so while I was off duty, I would drive to offenders' homes to ask them if they wanted to get off their drug of choice, which was usually heroin. I would offer transport for them to the hospital so that they could enter detox. Most times, these trips were pre-arranged but when I would turn up at their address, they would not be home. I also made up business cards with information about detox and drug rehabilitation and handed these out.

After returning to work for the first shifts after my former husband left me, I found out the name of the woman he left me for. Well, I immediately did unauthorised checks on her through the police computers. I'm not sure what I was looking for, but I was obsessed. In the back of my mind, I think I was worried about the environment my kids were going to be in, if the former husband would have weekend access to the children. Sadly, this was not to be — when he left me, he left the kids, too. For about a week I was running checks on this person, and it was consuming my every thought. Then came the guilt: what I was doing was unethical. So I got off my chair and walked into my boss's office. I admitted everything to him. He said, 'In all my thirty-something years of policing, I have never heard of a copper putting in a complaint about themselves.' I sat there while he completed a heap of paperwork. He told me that I would be contacted by someone from the Ethical Standards unit. I was facing possible demotion in rank, a pay cut, or worse, the sack. I was on tenterhooks for the next couple of months, until I was notified via email that a date had been set for an interview with Ethical Standards. On the day I was so nervous, but I shouldn't have worried: the sergeant who interviewed me was a good mate of mine, and he worded me up prior to the interview, which helped put my mind at ease. He told me not to say too much — short answers, yes or no — because at the end of the interview, he'd have to type it up, and he didn't want to be there all day.

The interview took place in the formal interview room; it was being recorded, just like when police interview a suspect. I saw the sergeant sitting there with reams of paper in front of him. Apparently, that was the hard copy of the checks I had conducted. I was embarrassed and ashamed of what I'd done. While the sergeant was questioning me, he was kicking my foot under the table every time I started waffling on and going beyond the 'yes' or 'no' answers I was meant to give. The interview didn't take long. I had to wait a month to find out the consequences of my actions. I was given a pay cut that lasted for six months, and my 'length of time' in the police force was shortened by a year. This shortening of time had no relevance to me at the time, but years later I would find out what it meant. Fast-forward to when I'd been in the job for ten years, and I wasn't given my ten-year medal. Receiving medals in policing is a big deal. Police get a ten-year medal, and an additional one for every five years after. It's not often that police are rewarded for doing their job, and because I was forced to retire just after my ten-year period, I would never receive it. Word also got around that I was the copper that put in a complaint against themselves, and I was a laughing stock. That's okay, though — at least I was sleeping at night. It is common knowledge within the job that police do unauthorised checks on people: their neighbours, their mates, their family, and even each other. One time when I was in the watchhouse, and there was nobody in the cells or pods, one of my mates was placing bets on who had the cleanest traffic record. There were about five of us, and he ran all our names through the system.

I struggled financially after my marriage broke down. I had to stop doing normal shifts and could do dayshifts only. This was so I could be home with my children at night, as they were too young to leave on their own, and they were grieving the loss of their father. I was losing up to $700 per fortnight. Our first Christmas after the separation, I was totally broke, and had no money for bills, let alone Christmas presents. I explained to my children that it was payday the following day, and they were so supportive and understanding. I promised them that I would make it up to them. Christmas morning arrived, and I had the day off work. From inside the house, I could hear other families and their children celebrating, and trying out their new Christmas presents. No doubt my children heard as well. We had almost no food in the house.

In fact, I was broke for a long time before and after Christmas.

On many occasions, I had to go to Cash Converters to get payday loans, which meant that when I did get paid, a huge portion would go to paying their interest rates. I was truly embarrassed about having to do this, and never more so than the time, a couple of days after getting a loan, I had to go to the shop in my capacity as a police officer. I had to go through their inventory of pawned items to check if they were stolen — and there were many, which I seized and returned to the rightful owners. I was hoping that the staff wouldn't recognise me. I also had to get food vouchers from St Vincent's and the Salvation Army just to get by, and even then we still ran out of food. It was a really difficult time in our lives, and I felt like an absolute failure to my children. I never wanted my children to go through what I went through as a child. Going to bed hungry is the worst. Having no support is the worst.

I would have also been homeless were it not for the fact that a mate of mine — also a police officer — had rented her house to me about a month prior to Christmas. She allowed us to move in without paying bond; no inspections, and no two-weeks rent in advance, which was just as well because I never had it anyway. I'd left the family home I had been sharing with my former husband before he left; I could have stayed there, but I didn't want to, and the rent was so high I wouldn't have been able to afford it on my own. I had given away all my furniture; I was starting a new chapter in my life and didn't want any reminders of him. Now, this may work if you have money to buy new stuff, but it was an expensive exercise for me! It was necessary, though — part of the healing process.

It was such a blessing that I was given the house to live in, and I absolutely loved her for that. The house was typical for the environment we were in — a big backyard and situated in a cul-de-sac. My mate had moved to Townsville to be with her husband, who was in the army. The day after we moved in, the neighbour from across the road came over and introduced herself. I thought, *that was quick*; we hadn't even unpacked the boxes. She looked a bit rough around the edges. She was younger than me, with three children: two primary school–aged boys and a little girl, who was a toddler. All our other neighbours were elderly, so the street was pretty quiet. I introduced myself and my children in turn. I never told her I was a cop. I generally didn't like people to know, especially when I was off duty.

After a week, I found out just who was living opposite me. Apparently, she and her boyfriend — the father of the children — had just been released from prison, having served a lengthy sentence for robbing a petrol station with a blood-filled syringe. A syringe filled with HIV-positive blood. They were both positive, as prior to their sentencing, they had been heroin users. Highly addicted and committing crimes to feed their habits. They had just got their children back as well, and this was their first home together since leaving prison.

I gave my children strict instructions to stay away from the children across the road: 'And when I go to work, you are to stay inside until I get home.' This mainly applied when I worked on weekends. I came home one afternoon after doing a morning shift, and what did I see as I pulled my car into the cul-de-sac? My youngest daughter playing handball on the road with the boys opposite us, and my two older children in the front yard with the neighbours, who were busy cooking a barbeque. When I got out of the car, I had no choice but to go over. My cover was blown. They would see my uniform. As I entered the yard, though, it was all smiles. This woman and her boyfriend have been my best neighbours to date: I got along with both of them, and she would often come over for a cuppa or I would go to theirs. We would talk for hours and hours as they both became my friends.

My kids loved them as well. They'd keep an eye on the kids when I was at work. Our friendship was going great, but then I noticed a change in their behaviour. They were hardly ever home, and when I did see them, they'd be wearing long sleeves in scorching temperatures. I knew they were covering up their track marks. One day I saw her with a T-shirt on and was discreetly trying to check her arms, but she had a Band-Aid on her forearm. I asked her what it was for, and she said she'd cut herself. I thought, *an odd place to cut yourself.* I hated being treated like an idiot.

They had people frequenting theirs at odd hours, and one time a guy pulled up in a stolen car. A close friend of hers was at the house all the time. She would drop my kids off to the railway station in the mornings and even buy them breakfast at the local McDonald's. She always had money on her. One time, I was really desperate for money, as I was broke until payday, so I asked my neighbour if she had any money to loan me. Her friend piped up and said, 'I'll give ya a loan, but you don't have to pay me back.' She gave me $50. I was so grateful.

Payday came, and I paid her back like I said I would. Unbeknown to me, she always had money because she was committing handbag snatches in the area, and even did it at my neighbours' boys' primary-school fete. Essentially, she gave me money from proceeds of her crimes. She was known to police for fraud offences, and would later become known as Australia's queen of con artists. She would commit crimes in wigs and sunglasses, disguising her identity, and even gained entrance to a police station by posing as a police officer. She, too, had served time in the women's prison, which is where she met my neighbour. Apparently, she also had a boyfriend who was a police officer. He was a detective in the CIB. They were on their way to a casino for a night out, and they stopped at a convenience store along the way. Using someone else's keycard, she made purchases and withdrew a substantial amount of money, which she and her boyfriend spent at the casino. He was sacked from the police as a result.

I had told my neighbours months and months earlier that if I ever got a whiff that they were back on the gear, then our friendship would be over. When it was confirmed, I ended the friendship and moved away. I still lived in the same suburb, though. They knew where I had moved to and every now and then, one of the boys would knock on my front door. They knew what police station I worked at, and they would leave notes attached to my windscreen for me to contact them. As difficult as it was, I just couldn't do it. I didn't want to jeopardise my job. It's been years since then, and I know that they both have been sent back to prison for other crimes. I feel bad about this now, and I know that I should have contacted them.

CHAPTER 20

Back to that Christmas day, though. Another mate of mine —
also a police officer, of Maori descent — had told me that if I
didn't have any plans for Christmas, we could come down to her
place to spend it with her family. I had told her I was struggling
in conversations we had, and I think she recognised what I was
going through.

She was very proud of her culture and heritage and was
very involved with her community. Each year on 6 February,
the indigenous people of New Zealand celebrate the day of the
signing of the Treaty of Waitangi in 1840. One particular year on
this date, my friend had come to work with traditional markings
on her chin. Mostly they are tattooed, but she had drawn it on
with a marker. She worked at a different police station to me but
on this day, we'd ended up at a big job together. An inspector
was also present. After the job had finished, I got a phone call
on my private phone from the inspector — he wanted to know,
'What the fuck was on her face and is it permanent?' I told him
that I didn't think it was permanent, and he replied, 'Thank fuck
for that.'

Christmas day arrived, and as I said, there was no joy in my house, and no food either. As the clock struck one in the afternoon on this scorching-hot summer's day, the kids and I were starving. I had beef mince for a meal for dinner but nothing for a lunch, let alone a Christmas lunch. All morning I kept the invite in the back of my mind, but I hadn't taken up the offer because I felt ashamed. Eventually, I decided to go to her house. I had never been there before, and I only had an address. The kids and I piled into the car and off we went. They were so excited about the prospect of having a feed. When we got there, their Christmas lunch was over and done with. They had put their remaining food in the fridge. My friend pulled it out and placed it on the table in the backyard. She sat there and watched me and the kids scoff it down. We must have looked like vultures. She also had a pool, so the kids went swimming. I will always remember what she did for us that day.

This was my life for a while: get paid, pay the rent, get food in the cupboard, and then be broke until the next payday. When I say food — I only had enough food for a meal for dinner. It was so stressful; I would have to go to work knowing that my children were going to school hungry. How they learnt anything at school is beyond me. I would always tell the kids: *tough times make you a better person*. I didn't even have money for their railway tickets to get to and from school most days. Something had to change.

In the police force, police officers have firearms training every six months. Towards the end of 2003, I had been in my then current role for a little over a year, and my six-monthly firearm training had arrived. I didn't mind going to touch up my skills.

Although we were trained to shoot at the area of the body where all the vital organs are, we were trained to eliminate the threat, not to kill, which I found odd because if you get shot in the vital organs, the likelihood of death is high. Sometimes, my shots would all be in small groupings in the designated area; the instructors would tell me to do head shots. I found that exciting. They would stand beside me and yell, 'Left eye, right eye, nose.' I felt like a fucking sniper.

On this day, I was training with a group of inspectors. Inspectors are highly ranked officers, and most junior officers were intimidated by their presence. Not me. As I lined up beside an inspector from my district, he asked how I was. Big mistake; I told him the ins and outs of a cat's arsehole. I explained that I was struggling with my pay just doing dayshifts, but I couldn't do nightshifts because my kids needed me at home. All he said was, 'Leave it with me.' I didn't know what he meant, and didn't think of it again, but I must have made an impression on him, because two days after firearms training, I was called into my boss's office. He told me that I'd been offered a position at another police station in a specialised area, and not only that — I would also go back on the normal pay-rate but still didn't have to do nightshift. I was elated, and quickly accepted the offer. In fact, the inspector was based at the new police station where I was going. We became good mates; I would go sit in his office for a yarn at least once a week, and he would make me a cuppa. He was probably the best inspector I met in the job. With the extra income, our lives got better.

The traffic branch was in the office next to ours. In my first year of policing, I had rotated through the traffic branch, along with other specialised units including the Child Protection unit and SOC. I particularly didn't like traffic. They had a reputation that they would book their own grandmothers just to give out a ticket.

I had only been there a short time and was still in financial hardship while playing catch-up on my bills. Which meant that while I was able to pay the rent, other important things had to suffer — for example, my car. All the tyres were bald, with wire sticking out of them, and for about a month, I was even driving my car unregistered. Before this, though, I was parked in the staff carpark one day when I got an email from a traffic cop, who advised me that my tyres were unroadworthy and needed to be attended to ASAP. Now for that officer to know this, they would have had to run my vehicle details through the police system and physically check the tyres on my car. Why were they doing that? Was I the only vehicle they put through the system? I *was* the only black cop. After this friendly email, I started parking my vehicle around the corner from the police station, to hide from the traffic unit, and walking the rest of the way to work until I could get it fixed.

My new boss didn't particularly like me, which was fine because I didn't like him. He was a chauvinistic pig whom we all called Chucky. In my newly appointed position, my role was pretty much a lot of paperwork and, in particular, serving paperwork, which meant I worked alone most shifts. The paperwork was 'notice of evictions' or, the official title, 'warrants of possession'. This is when landlords, either private or housing commission, go to court and get paperwork to officially evict their tenants. After the tenants have been served the paperwork, they have 14 days to leave the house, to vacate the premises. I would return to the same address, 14 days later, to make sure they'd vacated.

Ninety-nine per cent of tenants hadn't left, and I'd tell them they had to leave immediately with whatever possessions they could take. All the other furniture would be packed up and placed in storage containers by removalists, and if the tenant didn't come up with the money to pay the landlord for the transport and the storage fees within a certain time, then all items could be sold, and any monies given to the landlord for money owing. The system didn't make sense — how were they meant to come up with the money to pay for all that if they couldn't pay their rent?

Basically, I was kicking people out, and if anyone played up, I was to call for back-up on the police radio. I hated this aspect of the job. I felt hypocritical: here I was, barely scraping by, making just enough to pay the rent and the bills. I knew exactly what these people were going through. Not just when I was a police officer, but in my former life, too, when I was getting evicted. I never had to call for back-up, due to my experiences and my communication skills, I guess. It still hurt, though.

At this police station, there were a lot of stuck-up white cops. I didn't really make friends with anyone, except with an old boy who had been in the job since he turned 18. He was the same rank as me, whereas others he'd gone through the academy with were now ranked inspectors and above. He loved Aboriginal people and he loved women. I fit both these categories. He was the funniest person I had ever met in the job. I actually wondered how he stayed in the job for so long, because he did fuck-all work. He would come out in the police car with me, though, especially if our unit had to do some revenue raising. This happened about once a month. We were advised that we had to meet a quota of roadside breath tests and traffic infringement notices, and the only way he was going to do this was if he worked with me. I would get him to drive and tell him who to pull over. When we intercepted the vehicle, I would tell him to stay in the car while I did the work.

The other friends I made at this station were two Indian guys. They were pretty awesome; one had been shot at years earlier during a vehicle intercept, and the other — well, he just wanted to be there. The one that had been shot at was a property mogul and owned almost every house in a new estate built in the next suburb over. I never got on with the other officers. One of them even put in a complaint about me to the boss, saying that I was always leaving work early when I did a 'two to ten'. When I did these shifts, I usually worked on my own. So, I took to taking selfies with the wall clock to provide evidence of the time I ended my shifts. These white cops made it unbearable for me when the Palm Island riots were happening in November 2004. They made racist comments about Aboriginal people in earshot of me, and they wore wrist bands in support of the police officer who'd been charged with the death in custody. He was acquitted, as so many police are. Since the Royal Commission into Aboriginal Deaths in Custody report was completed in 1991, there have been a further 437 deaths, and no police have ever been made accountable. Their behaviour caused me so much anxiety; I told the boss about it, but he didn't do anything. I even told the Aboriginal and Torres Strait Islander worker in the ethnic and diversity unit based at police headquarters, who by now I had on speed dial. She came out to my station and pretty much advised me to quit the job. I didn't quit, though — I put the Aboriginal flag on my desk.

CHAPTER 21

I spent a lot of time driving from one address to another, serving paperwork or making an enquiry. One of the addresses I attended belonged to the family of one of the members of the infamous 'Bali Nine'. I had to serve paperwork to a family member. When I arrived at the house, there were about 20 people there and a strong smell of cannabis. I served the paperwork and drove off around the corner, where I got on the police radio, and asked for any available units to come help me conduct an emergent search. An emergent search is a search of a house or property without a search warrant, because applying for the search warrant will give the person time to get rid of the evidence. The police officer applies for the search warrant after the search.

I had holidays owing and decided to take my children to see my mum in Sydney. This was only the third time that my children had seen their grandmother. I was really worried that Mum wouldn't stick to her promise of no alcohol. To my surprise, she did, and we had the best time. It's a memory that I will always treasure. Back home, I returned to my routine — work and kids. By now, in 2005, I had been a police officer for three years and had undertaken studies to become a senior constable. I had also become a part of a specialised team, the Tactical Crime Squad(TCS), which was full of men. Our role within the police was to target drug and property offences. This included proactive-style policing, drug raids, patrolling the district and intercepting persons and vehicles, and conducting searches for drugs and stolen property. Nine out of every ten intercepts, I would find drugs, mainly heroin. This success came from gut feeling and experience.

You would be surprised where drug addicts would hide their heroin, ice, speed, and marijuana. During drug raids, I was like a sniffer dog — I could find drugs in the most obscure places. In the freezer, cereal boxes, and even attached to Blu-tack that was holding a poster on the wall. There was one drug house that if you raided on a Monday, by Tuesday, they were back in business. I have no idea what the dealer was doing to the heroin, but a lot of young people were overdosing after buying from this house. Some would even overdose in their front yard. I was fed up, so I started having my lunch at the front of their house while sitting in the police vehicle. It stopped their drug trade for a little while.

Police radios were once analogue but were changed to digital for security reasons. When it was an analogue system, people listened to us with their scanners, which made it hard when conducting raids, especially on large criminal groups. We would have to go to another radio channel. We called this the 'chatter channel'. Before going onto the chatter channel, you'd have to advise comms that you were doing so. Well, whenever anybody announced this, everyone in the district switched over as well, and would turn their handheld to the main channel. We'd hear police running down other officers back at the station. It bemused me that if this was how they treated their own, god help the general public.

There was one job I knew television cameras were going to be at. I think it was for *A Current Affair*. Information had come through Crime Stoppers that a driving-school instructor always smelt of alcohol when instructing learner drivers, and most of them suspected that he was drunk. This intelligence was given to the traffic branch in my district and assigned to a senior constable. He was flying solo that day and asked if I would be his partner for the filming of the arrest. He would be doing the arrest — all I would have to do was stand there. Easy. I did it, and then telephoned the family and told them to watch. The other times I saw television cameras at my jobs, I wasn't sure if I actually made it through the editing process. But sometimes I'd get phone calls from people saying that they had just seen me on the news. Obviously, this was for big jobs, like sieges and robberies.

On one occasion, I was the arresting officer at a siege. Uniformed officers from another police station attended an address in attempts to arrest a male resident, who was wanted on warrants. The house was an old Queenslander with stairs leading to the front door. There were also stairs at the rear of the house, leading to the back door, which was the main point of entry, as overgrown bushes had taken over the front. As the officers knocked on the back door, a male in his thirties answered, holding a sawn-off shotgun aimed at the officers. The officers ran back down the rear stairs — I'm pretty sure they skipped a few steps getting away! They got on the police radio and requested backup. Backup arrived and cordoned the house off, making sure the armed man didn't escape.

Unaware of what had unfolded, I had started my shift for

the day. Kitted up and announced my shift on police radio. I was working with my usual partner, who was also Aboriginal, and who was in the TCS with me. He was my best friend in the job, and we worked together for much of my time in the police. The thought of doing a shift with him was the main reason I turned up. The times I didn't work with him were on his days off; on those occasions I preferred to work on my own, as I didn't want to work with white cops.

The district duty officer phoned me and told me to go to the address and wait until the armed man surrendered, as I was to be the arresting officer. When we got there, we drove through the cordon and parked near the house. I got out of the car and walked to where the Special Emergency Response Team (SERT) boys were. This is the unit that attend high-risk jobs. There was a negotiator there as well, telling the armed man to come out of his house with his hands above his head, but to no avail. Negotiators are trained for situations like this. This went on for hours and hours, as sieges usually do. I've never been to a siege that ended quickly. I was anticipating *overtime, for sure* with this job, so I called the kids to let them know I was going to be late home, and to watch the news as I might be on there.

After hours without any response from the armed man, SERT threw a remote camera in a window at the side of the house. There was a screen inside the SERT van that relayed vision from the camera, which was being remotely controlled by a SERT officer. I was watching the screen when the armed man came into focus. He was on a lounge chair, fast asleep. SERT took this opportunity to bust down the back door and enter the house, disarming the man and bringing him outside to me. As he was led down the rear stairs, I was waiting for him with handcuffs at the ready. I arrested him and advised him of his rights.

I gloved up and grabbed the sawn-off shotgun, which I quickly saw was locked and loaded, ready to fire. I rendered it safe by removing the bullet, and then bagged it up as evidence. During a further search of the house, and under the house where there was a laundry and workshop area, I saw parts to other shotguns. When the matter went to court, he was deemed unfit to stand trial due to lack of mental capacity, so the matter was heard at the Mental Health Review Tribunal instead.

Before digital radio, the media and tow-truck companies had the pick of which jobs they wanted to attend and film. Whenever we got traffic-accident jobs, the tow trucks would get there before we did, and not just one tow truck, but several. They would hear the jobs coming over the radio. I went to a traffic accident once, and two men from two separate tow-truck companies were full-on fighting over who was getting the job. To settle the fight, I asked who got there first. *Right, it's your job*. Often, though, cars that had been in traffic accidents were still driveable, but the tow-truck drivers would convince the unsuspecting drivers that their cars were not fit or too dangerous to drive. So, I took it upon myself to check the vehicles and tell people to not have their car towed if it was driveable, as it would cost them hundreds of dollars in tow-truck fees. Whenever I turned up to traffic accidents, tow-truck drivers would roll their eyes in disappointment.

In another siege, close to where I was living, a naked man was running up and down the street with a firearm. Why he chose to do this naked is beyond me. My partner and I were given the job of sitting in the front yard of the house directly opposite the man's house. We watched him come in and out of the house, and onto the street, but without his weapon. He would come outside his house and yell. My partner and I were possibly the worst officers to be attempting stealth mode. We both smoked, and I have no doubt the naked man knew we were there, with the amber lights of our lit cigarettes and the smoke emitting from them.

In policing it often seems that certain people attract certain jobs; for example, I had a mate that almost every shift he worked, he got a dead body. For this reason, we referred to him as 'doctor death'. I was called the 'shit magnet'. Every shift I worked, shit would follow. I always had the big jobs, pursuits, and foot chases; I was always calling out 'urgent' on the police radio. This is the reason a lot of first year constables wanted to work with me — to gain more experience.

I remember one job when we were called to an affluent suburb due to a disturbance at the address. When we got there, a large man was screaming and yelling at us, almost incoherent, and then all of a sudden, he stripped off his clothing and jumped in the pool in the backyard. I just kept saying, 'Don't make me come in there to get you; now, get out!' I don't actually know what I was going to do if I did go in there. After some time, he came out of his own accord, but was putting up a fight as I was trying to handcuff him. He fell to the ground and I fell on top of him, slipping and sliding around. It wasn't funny at the time but afterwards, I laughed so much. It must have looked so funny.

I was also involved in the first torture case in the state. My involvement was minimal, but it still had a lasting impact. I was one of a few police officers that continually attended the address, all on callouts of a similar nature. The address was actually flagged in our system, which meant that whenever a job was called, more than one unit would attend, as the offender was known to be violent towards police.

The offences he committed were horrendous, and most of them were sexually gratifying to him. He was, and probably still is, a fucking animal. The case traumatised me, his victim, who was also his wife, and I'm sure other police involved. When it went to court, I sat for hours waiting to give evidence but was not required in the end. After the court case finished, I found out that the charge of torture was dropped, and he was charged with lesser charges. Torture is a hard charge to prove but carries a hefty sentence. It's often accompanied by other serious offences, like deprivation of liberty, grievous bodily harm, and attempted murder.

There was usually no debriefing involved for these jobs, and they were taking a toll on my mental health. I dealt with it as best I could — to some extent, you just switch off, data dump it, and go to the next job. But there are a lot of things that I saw while policing that I cannot remove from my memory. I remember sitting in a cordon along with other police while a 'doggie' — which is what we called a dog handler — was picking up the scent of an Aboriginal man who was wanted for a variety of offences and warrants. He was eventually located, so we all met up. The Aboriginal fulla was handcuffed with his hands behind his back, leaning against the police vehicle while other police stood around him. When the dog handler and his dog got there, the dog handler said something and then I saw the police dog lunge forward and bite the Aboriginal man's lower left calf. I saw blood, skin, muscle, flesh, and tendons hanging. I gasped in fright, but I provided him with first aid until the ambulance arrived, while he screamed in agony and the other white police laughed about it.

On Mother's Day weekend in 2007, I was working, and towards the end of my shift, a job came over the radio. A family with young children were celebrating Mother's Day by having a picnic beside the lake in my policing area. This lake was man-made, and developers had built housing estates around it. A young boy, aged three, had wandered off and couldn't be found by his parents. My heart sank. I was feeling so devastated that as I got home and pulled into my driveway, I couldn't shake this job off. I beeped my horn and the kids came outside. We drove for hours around the lake area, looking for the little boy. I was hoping that he had wandered off in the residential area or made his way to a playground, and, with increasing dread, I was hoping he wasn't in the lake. Hours went by without any sighting, so they called in police divers. They found the child in the lake, wedged against a rock. Possibly the worst Mother's Day. My heart went out to the family of the young child. I'm pretty certain that by exposing my own children to this, I may have caused them trauma. At the time, I was just thinking it was our duty to try to find this young boy.

It was during this time that I began to realise I was taking a downhill spiral. I'd lost the ability to switch off. I had never wanted to be one of those cops — the ones that flash their badges when they are off duty, on their own little power trips. Speaking to people like they were on a job. I saw this happen to police officers around me — like the female cop who had just been transferred to our district, and who was out walking in a local park near her home when she saw a man with two dogs that were off the leash. She approached this man and started preaching about the rules of the park; she told him she was a police officer, and that if he didn't put the dogs on the lead, then she would be forced to act. The man identified himself as an inspector — technically, her superior. Not long after this, she was transferred out of the district.

CHAPTER 22

Throughout my policing, I maintained rapport with the Aboriginal community, and every now and then, I would attend the juvenile justice detention centre to speak to the young Aboriginals, to explain to them what their rights and responsibilities were when they were approached by police. I was also given the grand tour of this barbaric institution, which saddened my heart, because those children didn't belong there. Prior to attending, I had been warned that these youth have a tendency to be violent and rude to police, all with good reason. This never fazed me, though, and by the end of my sessions with the youths, they were often hugging me and calling me aunty.

I also did a few stints at the watchhouse — usually so that I could have a break from being on the road. In my policing area, the watchhouse used to be within a police station, but a new one had been built under the new Magistrates Court. When it was at the police station, it had up to four cells that housed up to ten people at any given time, but the new one housed five times as many. At the old cells, you had to walk up the corridor every five to ten minutes to conduct observations on the people in the cells, but the new one had state-of-the-art surveillance. There were cameras in the old cells, but they had dried-up toilet paper and faeces on them, and you could barely see anything. The new cells were called pods, and each had a built-in television. The showers and toilets were controlled by officers with a click of a button. On the screen, we could monitor all pods at once. One time, while I was monitoring the pods on the screen, I saw a man pissing on the floor of the common area instead of in the toilet. I let my colleagues know what I had just seen, and all of a sudden, one of the male officers walked in there, picked the man up, and drove him straight into the brick wall, headfirst. I heard an almighty crack. The officer slammed the pod-door shut, and we never mentioned it again. The officer knew that I saw this as well, but he didn't care, and why would he? These occurrences were common, but no complaints were ever made. White cops know they can pretty much get away with anything and they do. These were the jobs that tore me up inside. What little tolerance I had for white cops was diminishing; I often hated being a cop, and I hated them even more.

As well as monitoring and signing in new arrests, we had other duties at the watchhouse. One of them was to drive to the prisons to pick up prisoners who had court that day. This was called transport duties. We had to go to the men's jail, the women's jail, and the protection prison. This last one housed people who were unable to be housed in mainstream jails, either due to the crimes that they'd committed or to who they are. So, they usually housed paedophiles — who were called rock spiders — sex offenders, and police officers. At the time, I knew of about ten former police officers being held for crimes they had committed while they were cops.

The prison van could carry up to ten prisoners at any time, to and from court. They were seated in single seats, each of which had a caged door that was locked, and then the sliding door of the van would also be closed. So they were very secure, and all prisoners would be handcuffed prior to the transport. I used to hate going to the men's prisons; I always felt frightened. These guys were huge compared to my little frame. If they wanted to hurt me, they could have, but they never did. I don't think any amount of police training would have saved me if they'd assaulted me. I never had a firearm on me, because when you worked in the watchhouse, no firearms were permitted. When you arrived back at the watchhouse, you'd drive up to the roller-door entry, which staff would open remotely, and then drive the van inside a holding area. You wouldn't let anyone out of the van until the roller door had fully closed behind you.

One time, I was working with a sergeant who didn't usually do watchhouse or transport. I had no idea why he was doing it on this particular day, but I should have looked at it as a sign of shit to come. Actually, come to think of it now, I had never seen this sergeant do any form of police work. He may have been just waiting for retirement. He was not someone other officers took seriously; he was laughed at behind his back. One of the things he was mocked for was this time he was travelling to work on the train. Apparently, he used to drive his Holden sedan to the carpark of a railway station, where he'd leave it for the day while he travelled by train to work. The car was a dump — I don't think it could have made it all the way to the police station and back. I truly don't know how it passed its roadworthy. Well one day, the good sergeant was seated on the train as it travelled alongside a freeway, and what did he see? His own car being driven on the freeway, travelling in the same direction as him. I was patrolling the area in a police vehicle when the job came over the radio. We all pissed ourselves laughing.

So on this day, there was a big case being heard: a murder trial that was being heard in the Magistrates Court, before it moved to the District or Supreme Court, in the city. In other words, a court process before all evidence is presented in the big courts. But the justice system being what it is — often a waste of time and resources — all offenders and witnesses were required before the Magistrates Court. We only had to pick up and transport two male prisoners: one was from the mainstream jail and the other from the protection jail. The guy from mainstream was the main offender, and the one from protection was a witness. We were told to keep these two separated at all times, and not to let the main offender see the witness. Prior to leaving the watchhouse, we'd hatched a plan to put the witness in cell A and the offender in cell B. The witness was to move away from the door, so that the offender — who was a bikie from a well-known bikie gang — wouldn't see him.

So off we went, to the protection prison first and then to the mainstream jail. Once we got back to the watchhouse, the sergeant unlocked the padlock and released the offender first, all while the roller door was still open. Not only was he not sticking to the plan, but he'd taken off the prisoner's handcuffs before he was placed in the cell. Then, before I could say anything, he put the bloody witness in with the offender. He didn't take the handcuffs off the witness either, and once they were alone, all hell broke loose. The witness didn't stand a chance, and officers entered and quickly removed him to another cell. The offender was still causing havoc, so the officers asked him to come to the door and place his hands through the opening to be handcuffed again. He wouldn't, and when an officer entered the cell to handcuff him, the offender attacked. This guy was a machine. He threw punch after punch at the officer. A full-on fist fight ensued, and there was blood dripping and the thuds of body blows. Other officers had to go in to help our fellow watchhouse member, who by now was all busted up. Just like on the road — there was never a dull moment in the watchhouse.

There was no action taken against the sergeant over this. There never was.

The TCS members were like brothers to me. We were a tight-knit group until we got a new member, J., in 2008. I took a dislike to him immediately, especially when he said in front of me that there was no place for females in the police. I also sensed that he didn't like Aboriginal people. I reminded him that police should represent the community, and that the community isn't just made up of white people. I refused to work with this member, except for on one occasion, when I had no choice.

Many times, I received phone calls from the partners or wives of male Aboriginal offenders, who were wanted by police for outstanding warrants or for recent crime sprees committed to support drug habits. My other teammates would want my informants' details, but I would never give them out, as I knew that I would be breaking the trust that I had with my contacts. One particular shift, I was trying to catch up on my paperwork, when I received a phone call from the girlfriend of an offender who was wanted by police. She told me where I could find him right at that minute. So, armed with this information, I gathered a team up — including J. — and went to the address. Sure enough, as we exited our vehicles, the offender ran out of the rear door of the property and scaled the back fence into the neighbour's yard. A few of the boys jumped the fence, while I got back into the vehicle and drove around the corner to the yard that the offender was last seen in. As I arrived, I saw J. drag the offender from under a car in the driveway, handcuff him, and then kick him in the head with his work boots. I saw teeth and blood spill from his mouth. I was horrified and angry — I had been trusted to bring in the offender unharmed. I got on the police radio and requested an ambulance to attend the address, because the offender was unconscious and non-responsive. By the time the ambulance arrived, he was responsive, and was never taken to hospital; they just assessed him and deemed him fit to go to the watchhouse, where he was charged and remanded in custody. While I was with the offender in the ambulance, I could see J. sitting on the front step of the house, hyperventilating and holding his chest. He told me he thought that he was having a heart attack. The ambulance ended having to transport *him* to hospital instead. Protocol and common sense dictate that when one of your fellow officers go to hospital, you usually follow in the police vehicle and sit with your mate until seen by the doctor. I was so angry with J. that I didn't follow the ambulance to the hospital; I went to the watchhouse with the offender instead. When I returned to the station, I reported what had happened to my officer in charge. This complaint went nowhere; for one, I think he was uncomfortable putting forward my complaint because I was a woman, but it's also rare to put in formal complaints against a fellow officer.

I went home at the end of my shift, still upset by what had occurred. In the morning, I drove my personal vehicle to the watchhouse to see the offender. He had dried blood around his mouth and teeth missing. I asked if he was okay and told him to make a complaint about police brutality and to give my name as the witness. He never did, and I haven't heard from or seen him again. This behaviour in policing is quite common, but the general public don't often hear about it.

CHAPTER 23

Other than when I had to deal with dead bodies on the job, I can recall two other times that I cried. I'm not sure if that was because I'm a mother or if it was a cultural thing — all I know is that these two particular jobs are still vivid in my memory. The first was when I received a job to attend an address to conduct a welfare check on three young children who were in the care of their mother. The job had been placed by the Department of Families (now the Child Safety Department), which had received complaints of neglect, and wanted welfare to check on the kids. Apparently, department social workers had been attending the address for weeks, but each time, the mother and children were not home. According to legislation, if the department is unable to conduct their assessment, then police are able to, and can remove children if deemed necessary. On this particular shift, I was working alone, and received the job because they had information that the mother was at home.

I drove to the address in question, and when I arrived it was getting on dark, and I could see lights on inside the house. I walked up the staircase to the front door and knocked. I was soon greeted by a young woman in her early twenties. I introduced myself and explained why I was there. She allowed me in, although I don't think she realised that she had no choice. With or without her permission, I was entering her house that late afternoon.

When I got into the lounge room, I saw the three children I had to conduct an assessment on. They were all under five years old, their little faces looking at me, with blonde hair and big blue eyes. At the time, I didn't know exactly what I was looking for. *How will I know if the children are being neglected?* It reminded me of the time when my three children were all under five, the youngest a newborn. I was living on my own with them at the time, and had made up mattresses on the lounge-room floor for us all to sleep on. I was lying on the mattress, breastfeeding my new bub, when there was a knock on the front door. I got up to answer it and saw three white people standing on my front porch. They said that they had received complaints and needed to check on my children. I asked them what the complaints were, but they wouldn't tell me. I asked them to wait while I made a phone call, and telephoned my father, who at the time was working for the same department but in a different location. He asked to speak to them, I handed them the phone, and that was that — the white people on the porch left. I got back on the phone to my father and asked him what he'd told them; he said that I was a good mother and that the complaints they'd received were false and malicious. He also told me that I still needed to comply with their assessment by taking the kids into their office the following day. I was so upset that someone could make false claims about my mothering.

The following day, I drove my children to the Department of Welfare, Child Safety so that the assessment could be done. I explained to the two bigger children that some people were going to speak to them and maybe ask them some questions, and that they didn't need to be frightened. I pulled up out the front, got the children out, and carried my newborn baby in her car capsule. When I got into the front foyer, I was met by one of the white people who'd visited the previous day. She told me that I could stay where I was with the newborn, but she needed to take the two bigger children with her. I asked her where she was taking my children and if I could be with them, and she told me that she would be doing a strip search of my children. Apparently, they were looking for bruising on the children's bodies. I was shocked; I couldn't understand why anybody would say that I would harm my babies. I was visibly upset by now. I tried not to cry in front of the bigger kids, though, as I wanted them to be brave and go with the white lady without me.

Five minutes passed, then the lady returned with my children. We went into an office. She told me that the complaint was closed, as she'd found no evidence to support it. I asked her where the complaint came from — expecting her not to tell me due to confidentiality — but she blurted out that it had come from a relative of my ex-partner, the father of my son and newborn daughter. I was even more shocked when I heard this. I'd never got along with his family, but I didn't think that they would do this. The lady told me that if they received any more complaints, they were going to ignore them. A mixture of emotions that day. Shocked, upset, terrified, and — most importantly — relieved. Relieved that the kids and I would never have to go through this again. So, I knew exactly how this young mother felt the day I went into her house.

I walked around the house; I could see toys scattered on the floor, and beds were unmade, but there was nothing to alarm me.

I walked back into the lounge room and sat next to the mother, who was holding her baby. He had rosy-red cheeks and the biggest blue eyes I had ever seen on a baby. I changed his nappy and noticed that he had a nappy rash, but other than that, he appeared to be fine, as were the other children.

I left the house, returned to my police station, and telephoned the welfare officer with the results of my assessment. End of the job and end of my shift. I was excited because I had been working ten days straight and was getting five days off. I couldn't wait to get home to my kids.

The next morning, I was awoken by my mobile phone ringing. When I answered it, the boss of my police station was on the other end. I immediately thought, *this can't be good.* Your boss never rings you when you're on a day off unless it's urgent. Like 'you're required to give evidence in court' urgent. He told me that the baby had died at the house I'd been to the night before, and I needed to come into the station immediately. I lost control of myself; I was sobbing. I got up out of bed, and got dressed, and drove to my station through tears.

I was terrified. I started to wonder what I had missed at the house, why the baby had died. *I should have removed the children. Should've would've could've.* Then, selfishly, I started to stress that I was going to get the sack and lose my career and my income. I cried for the mother, I cried for the poor defenceless baby, and I cried for myself.

When I got to the station, there were inspectors everywhere. I was told that I needed to complete a statement as soon as possible about my time in the house, my observations, conversations I'd had with the mother, and, most importantly, the condition of the baby at the time and my reasons for not removing the children.

Halfway through the statement, my boss informed me that a post-mortem was being conducted on the baby as we were speaking, and that we'd know the results soon. I continued with my statement; it was hard to do, and I kept thinking of his rosy cheeks and his blue eyes. I needed a break and went to the designated smoking area at the back of my station. I lit up a smoke, and then a plain-clothes officer led some people to where I was so that they could have a smoke as well. It turned out that they were the family of the baby. I couldn't look them in the eye. I quickly drew on my cigarette, and went back inside to finish the statement. When I'd completed it, I gave it to my boss, and told him I would wait to hear the autopsy results. About an hour later, results in: the baby had died of cot death. I was told that whether I'd removed the children or not, the baby still would have died. I never felt relieved, though — I was just sad that a little life had been lost, and for the pain that the mother must be feeling.

The other job that reduced me to tears was a few years after this in 2009, when I received a job to attend an address to remove two children from the parents. No assessment was required, as this had already been conducted by welfare, and it had been to court. So, with court order in hand, I went to the house with the sergeant I was working with that day.

When we got there, I saw a small boy, naked, playing in the dirt in the front yard, and a little girl about five years old sitting on the step to the front door. We got out of the police car and walked to the house. Their mother and father were sitting in the lounge watching television. It appeared that they had been expecting our arrival because they didn't seem surprised. We explained why we were there and handed them the court order. They scurried around the house, gathered what little clothing the children had, and politely handed the children to us, waving to them as we placed them in the back of the police vehicle.

Off we drove to a family group home, where a complete stranger was now to care for the two children until the next court date, where the parents would have to prove their fitness to parent. The little boy, who was dressed now, was quiet and never said much, but the five-year-old girl was so talkative and had an old soul for her age. She was asking us questions about where we were taking her and her brother, why couldn't she stay with her mum and dad. She started to cry and say she wanted to go home, so I sang to her; I think it was a kid's song, because I remember that she started singing with me in her cute little voice. As I was singing, silent tears ran down my face. That day, I cried for the children.

These jobs not only reminded me of the time I'd had dealings with welfare, but also reminded me that my grandmother had been forcibly removed and separated from her mother and siblings, and that my father, when he was a young boy living on the mission, would have to run into the bushes and hide whenever they heard vehicles driving along the dirt road into the mission. He'd have to stay in thick scrub until he was told to come out.

The stolen generation. How ironic that during that bleak period, white people were removing black children, and here I was: a black police officer removing white children.

The pain and suffering of the stolen generations is passed down from generation to generation. My grandmother lived this fear, my father experienced the fear, and I feared the experience. I have passed this down to my children through the stories that were told to me, and that I told them in turn. There were a lot of days when I wanted to quit the police. There were things I heard and saw that made me regret becoming a police officer. One particular day, in March 2006, was one of those dark days. Three young Aboriginal boys were killed while playing on a suburban railway track. The oldest boy was ten and the youngest was eight. They were two brothers and a cousin.

Apparently, a call came in that these boys had climbed through a hole in the fence on the side of the tracks and were playing around and throwing rocks. I'm not sure how this job was detailed, but I know that a single officer from the railway squad attended and spoke to the boys. Police officers from the railway squad generally ride the trains, and they mainly deal with offences in relation to fare evasion.

This police officer — whom I know personally — got back on the next train and carried on with normal duties. Within minutes, another job came through the police radio — three boys hit and killed by a train.

I'm not drawing a comparison to the young boys that were killed, but when my son was 15 years old, he was at a railway station, and had no money nor a ticket for the train. He was sitting on the platform when he was approached by two police officers who asked him to show them his railway ticket. My son told them he didn't have one. They issued him with a fine on the spot.

I only heard about this when he came home with the fine. Police officers have a duty of care when dealing with young people and certainly with vulnerable people. Their duty of care required them to call or make contact with a parent — me — in relation to my son attempting to catch a train without a ticket. Or they should have driven him home. But no; instead they issued an infringement notice, knowing full well that a 15-year-old would not be able to afford this sort of payment in the time frame that repayment was expected. I wrote a letter of complaint, outlining my concerns and the failure of duty of care that day, and the fine was revoked.

That day on the railway track, when the police officer was speaking to those three young boys, he should have taken them home or asked for the assistance of an Aboriginal Police Liaison Officer or requested backup from other police officers in the area. According to the officer — in evidence he gave during the subsequent coronial inquest — he believed that if further action had been taken with these boys, they would have run. Hindsight is a beautiful thing, but surely common sense must prevail, and a duty of care should have been followed. During the coronial inquest, the coroner described the train driver as 'driving dangerously', but he has never faced any criminal charges. As for the police action that day — or lack of — the coroner ruled that there was no wrongdoing.

I am sure that if these young boys had not been Aboriginal, and had been white kids, the outcome would have been completely different.

It has been over ten years since this happened, and I still have sleepless nights.

CHAPTER 24

The events that would have such a huge impact on the rest of my life happened in 2008. I was driving through a suburb when I heard a call on the police radio: 'Any unit, Code 2, robbery in progress.' The address of the robbery happened to be a jewellery shop. I knew other police would be driving to the location of the robbery, but I knew that the offender would have already gone. Even better — police communications announced that the offender had taken off on foot, and they gave the direction of travel on the radio. I drove to where I thought I would run if I was the offender. The off streets. I parked the police vehicle, and who should run around the corner? The offender. I engaged in foot pursuit — I was running in yards, jumping fences. At one stage, the guy got stuck, hanging upside down on a fence; I tried climbing over it but injured my knee. He freed himself and took off. I lost sight of him but knew he wouldn't have got too far. I was calling out my location as I was running after him, so, along with the other police, we set up a cordon until the dog unit arrived. When they arrived, the dog picked up a scent immediately. They found the guy in a barrel with the lid on in a backyard, along with heaps of jewellery. I limped back to my vehicle, went back to the police station and told my boss, 'I think I've damaged my knee.' He ordered me to go to the doctor up the road. I had X-rays on my knee that revealed that I had torn ligaments. I was in physio for weeks after this, but still went to work on light duties.

Another day, I was working a morning shift, and was sitting at the computer doing my paperwork. Another officer in my squad was working with a first year constable who was completing her rotation through our unit as part of her competency, but the officer had to dash out to court to give evidence. So, I was doing my paperwork, but I could see the first year constable looking bored, so I kitted up and took her out on the road. We were out no longer than five minutes, patrolling the streets, when a 'robbery with violence' job came through the police radio, a short distance from us. From the status of other police units in the area, it appeared that they were all tied up with other jobs, so we got on the radio and informed police communications that we could attend. The job came in as a routine job, a Code 3, which meant no lights and sirens, no urgency. As we approached the job location — the local Centrelink office — I could see a lot of people standing outside the office block. It turns out that during this incident, Centrelink had decided to do a fire-alarm check, a fire drill, so all staff and clients were outside.

I parked the police vehicle in front of the office block, directly in front of the steps leading to the entrance door. My partner and I got out and were walking up the steps to the building when I saw a young female, who appeared to be drug-affected, carrying handbags and laptop computers under her arm. Another female at the top of the steps was yelling, 'That's her!'

By this time, I was directly in front of the offender, and I grabbed her, which made her drop everything she was carrying on the ground. I placed her arms behind her back and advised her that she was under arrest. I shoved her up against the railings of the steps, and she put up a fight, but I had her contained. While I was doing this, I noticed that the first year constable was standing a couple of steps higher than me, and asked her to handcuff the offender, as my hands were occupied. I could see my partner trying to get her handcuffs out of the handcuff pouch that was attached to her utility belt; she appeared to be tugging and struggling. She yelled, 'I can't get them out,' so I manoeuvred my right hand around the offender's wrists to hold her, while with my left hand I reached for my handcuffs. I did this without looking, because after being in the job for so long, you get to know where all your accoutrements — your firearm, your handcuffs, your retractable baton — are. It becomes second nature. So, I had grabbed for my handcuffs when, all of a sudden, the female offender slid down and freed herself from my grip.

She grabbed my hair with such force that she pulled out clumps of it. The pain was intense. I tried desperately to free myself, but she kept pulling. I had to bring myself closer to her to reduce the pain I was feeling. But each time I pulled myself closer she was trying to grab my firearm from its holster on my right hip. I kept manoeuvring so that she couldn't get to my firearm and started upper-cutting her with my right fist. The blows were connecting with her face and head, but she didn't seem to feel them.

My partner was standing to my right; I was yelling at her to use her capsicum spray. I repeated this a few times. It's amazing what happens when your body is under such extreme pressure. Everything seemed to be moving in slow motion. Every movement, every thought. In this moment, I saw my partner extend her arm, and I could see the canister of capsicum spray in her hand, but nothing was coming out. I didn't know how long I could endure the pain. Then my thoughts moved to my loved ones: my three children and the new man I'd just started courting. Would I see them again? Was this the last job I'd ever do as a copper? Who would look after my children? The loves of my life.

I realised that if I didn't end the altercation, she would seriously injure me. I reached for my capsicum-spray canister, and once I had it, I released the lever and sprayed until there was no more to spray. I could see — through a cloud of burning mist — that it was working. The woman loosened her grip on my hair. With every ounce of energy I had, plus a burst of pure adrenalin, I threw the offender to the ground and handcuffed her.

My eyes were stinging, and I realised that I had sprayed myself in the process. Somehow, I pushed through the stinging of the eyes and the pain in my back. I saw other police vehicles arrive and felt an instant feeling of relief. I knew that we would be okay. One of my mates from the squad ran to me and could see that I was in discomfort. He took me to the bathroom inside the building and helped splash cold water over my eyes to relieve the pain.

When I got back outside, I could see that other police were loading the offender in the back of a police van to be taken to the watchhouse, where she would be formally charged with robbery with violence and with the assault on me. With my hair all over the place and my uniform soaking, I approached the first year constable and asked her what had happened. She told me that her handcuffs were stuck in the pouch, and that she'd been trying to use the capsicum spray, but nothing was coming out. I asked her to show me what she'd been doing, and she was holding the canister all wrong. Her thumb wasn't on the lever so it couldn't press down to make it spray.

I had really needed her during the struggle with the offender and she wasn't there for me. We drove to the watchhouse in silence, and I could feel every bump in the road because my back was killing me. After the watchhouse, we returned to the station. I was still pissed off with the first year constable, and I told her to go home. I was driven to hospital by other police to be checked over. I had to get X-rays of my back, which showed that I had slipped a disc.

I ended up being on light duties for a few weeks after this, too, which meant I couldn't go on the road, but instead had to stay in the police station to do desk duties. It was during my desk duties that I started feeling really down and isolated. I was in a dark place. I would get startled by loud sounds, and I was becoming very jumpy. I would go into the bathroom at work and cry, but no one knew. At home every night, I was having vivid nightmares from which I'd wake up screaming. I never spoke to anybody about how I was feeling. Police are meant to be strong and resilient, and there is a strong culture in the police that if you speak to a psychologist or anyone about your inner feelings, you are weak. No one wants to be a weak copper.

To add insult to injury, I was not getting the proper rest that I needed in order to fully recover. While at home, police would call me asking me for information about the whereabouts of certain criminals. One day in particular, a prolific criminal — who was well known to me — jumped out of an open window on the second level of a police station to escape custody while handcuffed, and the police called me about it. It didn't matter what time of day or night it was. Then when I was at work and supposed to be doing desk duties, they would send me out to conduct covert and surveillance work on suspected drug dealers

— and not just low-level drug dealers, either, but ones who were carrying guns.

I thought the only way I could get through this was to transfer to a quieter area, possibly a safer area to police in. I also wanted to continue my studies and assessments to become a sergeant. On impulse — without thinking and without speaking to my children about it — I applied for a position in the far north of the state, on the southern tip of the Cape York Peninsula.

To my surprise and my bewilderment, I was offered the transfer. I drove home and told my kids and my partner. My partner is a former soldier in the Australian Army. He had served in Timor and was in the army for eight years as a bombardier. We spoke at length about it, and with much trepidation, I accepted the transfer. My two oldest children decided that they didn't want to come with me: my oldest had just started a new job and my son was in his final year of high school. My youngest daughter and partner would come with me to my new location, while the two older children would stay behind in the house.

CHAPTER 25

I was given my start date at the new police station, and we packed up, and off we drove. Every mile, my heart felt heavier. What had I done? I had abandoned my two older children. Left them in a city to fend for themselves. These thoughts still haunt me today.

As we drove north of the city, the flora and fauna began to change dramatically. We stopped several times and stayed overnight in accommodation to recoup our energy. A few days later, we arrived, but there was no yippee or yahoo to greet us — there was just silence. I was given a new three-bedroom house, rent free. But my sadness overshadowed any joy I could be feeling. My thoughts kept returning to the children I had left behind. I wanted to just get into the car and drive back.

My first shift, I walked proudly into my new police station. It was a world away from where I had just come from, but I was adamant that I was going to give it a go and do my best — not only as a police officer to serve the community but also to fit in with my new colleagues.

It took me every ounce of strength and determination to go to work every day. The anxiety I had before every shift was numbing and almost paralysing. It wasn't that I feared what lay ahead in the job itself; it was working among white people, being the minority. Culturally different in every aspect. On days that it became too overwhelming, I stayed home and called in sick.

The day I began, two other new police officers were starting as well. It was comforting to know that I wasn't the only person feeling like it was their first day of school. As I entered the rear entrance of the police station, I was greeted by the officer in charge, who seemed to be very welcoming and friendly. Then I saw some other police officers sitting around, so I made my way around the room and introduced myself, knowing full well that they knew all about me. It's general practice to conduct checks and enquiries when you get a new officer to your station, just so you know who and what to expect. I wasn't concerned by this: I had the highest arrest rate for a female police officer in the region that I had just come from and coming from a TCS — which is an elite squad — was even better.

The officer in charge showed me around the police station, which didn't take long, and he also told me — in a nonchalant way — that there had been a recent sighting of a three-metre carpet python in the station, and that he didn't know where it was now. *Could this get any worse?* I have a phobia of snakes and all reptiles. Big or small. This took me back to some of the drug raids I had participated in during my career. We would smash our way into a house to gain entry, and I would then run through the house, gathering all the occupants, handcuffing them, and leading them to the lounge room of the house. Then, out of the corner of my eye, I would see pretty fish tanks, and on closer inspection realise that these pretty fish tanks contained snakes. I would slither my way out of the house as quickly as I could, and refuse to go back inside.

The officer in charge pointed out which desks I could take. I chose one and sat down in front of the computer. I did a quick scan for the snake and then placed my backpack on the floor next to my feet. This backpack was nothing special, but it had significance to me. I'd had it for years, from my very first day as a police officer up until now. Inside this backpack, I carried everything required for me to perform my duties. I unzipped it and carefully removed a framed photo of my three children. This photo has taken pride of place at every desk that I have ever sat at. Not only do my kids look beautiful in this photo, in their matching light-blue school uniforms, but it constantly reminded me why I was a police officer, and also that it was only a job. My real work was at home with them.

Time appeared to be going really slowly. The silence was almost deafening, and I began to feel bored. It was either sit around pretending to look busy or jump into the deep end. I got up from my desk and announced that I was going to go out on patrol, and asked who wanted to come out with me. As I scanned the room, I realised I didn't have many to choose from. It was the new cop to the station or the other new cop to the station —only new police officers were rostered on that shift. I chose the one closest to me. I put my heavy utility belt around my waist, and, with a huge sigh, I placed my loaded firearm into the holster, all the while thinking, *this is not a good start*. On my first day, I would have preferred to work with someone who had been policing there for a while. Someone who knew the area. Someone who knew the layout of the town. Someone who knew the trouble spots. Just someone other than the officer I was about to walk out with. I thought about who did the roster in the station, and why they would roster all the new officers to work together on their first shift. It didn't make sense to me. So off we went, out the rear door of the police station, and I clambered up into the passenger side of the police 4WD. The blind leading the blind.

This was a new experience for me, working in such a remote area and in a 4WD. The other cops at the station would make fun of me because I hadn't driven a 4WD before. Back where I had just come from, there were only police sedans and police motorcycles. My new partner and I drove around the township aimlessly, not sure where we were going, but I figured, *what better way to learn our new area than to get lost?* The roads were wider than I was used to, and there was a lot more dirt, but the town was pretty, as it sat along a crocodile-infested saltwater river.

I asked my partner to start intercepting random vehicles so that I could conduct licence checks and breath tests. The first vehicle we stopped delivered my first arrest in the new town. The charges were minor, but it felt good to get the monkey off my back. We returned to the police station and clocked off for the day. I drove home — which only took about three minutes, so there was no time to reflect on the day or even to think of what to have for dinner that night. I really didn't have much to say about my first day. All I could think was that I'd made a huge mistake and couldn't see how it could get any better. I think I cried myself to sleep that night; if I didn't, I probably should have.

By the end of the week, I had met all the other police officers in the station. Every shift, I would walk in and greet everybody, making my presence known, but I wasn't receiving the same in return. It was almost solemn. Nobody would speak to me unless I spoke to them; even then, they would keep it to one-word replies. Then one of the officers was having a barbeque at their house, and I decided *what better way to get to know my fellow officers?* At the end of the shift, I collected my intimate partner and daughter, and we drove to the officer's house on the outskirts of town. I thought that the party could be the icebreaker. A chance for my family to meet the people I was working with, and a chance to make new friends. The house was lit up, and I could hear talking and laughter as we exited the family car. We made our way to the rear of the house, and I introduced my family to the other officers. From then on, nobody spoke to us. I felt so embarrassed and angry, and most of all, I felt black. We soon left, and I apologised to my family for putting them through that. Unless you are black or from a minority group, it is difficult to understand how it feels, but I can tell you that it's the loneliest feeling. After almost every shift I went home crying, and I found it very hard to go back the next day.

This officer in charge and the other police at this station would have staff meetings and deliberately exclude the two Aboriginal Liaison Officers. I asked why they weren't there and was told that they didn't want them to know stuff, and, in particular, where they were planning to set up roadside breath testing during the next shift. They said that they would go and tell their families.

This continued for weeks at the station, but I still attended every shift as rostered. Then one night, during a shift, the police station received a direct call from the publican of the local hotel in town, explaining that a brawl was taking place just outside the hotel, and several people were involved. We travelled the three blocks to the job and got out of the vehicle. My partner was caught in the melee, so I pushed people away, protecting my partner from any potential dangers. We told people to leave and were speaking to the remaining people about what had taken place. I was speaking to a group of females on the footpath when suddenly all I could see were headlights coming straight for me, and I could hear the sound of a car accelerating. I pushed the women out of the way to avoid them being struck by the vehicle, and then I dived to get away as well. I got up and dusted myself off. I looked around, but the vehicle had travelled away. Then I saw its brake lights come on, and the car turned around and drove at me again. I pulled my firearm out of the holster, with the full intention to shoot the driver to avoid being hit, but then I recognised the vehicle. It had been parked at the hotel during the brawl, and I'd seen a small child in the rear seat. This stopped me from firing my weapon.

The driver skidded to a halt, and my partner and I ran to the driver's side of the vehicle, removed the female driver, and arrested her. As I handcuffed her, she was laughing. We transported her to the police station, where she was formally charged and placed in the cells to wait for court the following morning. I finished my shift and went home. I told my partner what had happened and cried all night. This crying continued for weeks; then came the nightmares, and I would wake up to find myself running up the hallway of the house. I wasn't sure what was happening to me, but I was frightening my family, in particular my daughter. I had days off from work and would send her to school, then, within an hour of her being at school, I would call her mobile phone, telling her to come home as I couldn't be on my own.

With much persuasion, I went to the doctor and told him everything. He immediately referred me to a psychiatrist and a psychologist at the local hospital. My behaviour was becoming more erratic, and at times I felt suicidal. I thought that the only way I could make things better was to not be there at all. I couldn't even put the uniform on and go to work. I felt like I was letting everyone down.

After my first appointment with the specialist, which involved much talking and sobbing, I was diagnosed with post-traumatic stress disorder (PTSD). I felt so relieved that there was a name for what I was going through. The specialist filled out medical forms with strict instructions to stay home from work and to attend appointments with him regularly, as well as a prescription for medications. My partner took my medical certificate to my boss at the police station while I was at home. It took me weeks to leave the house, and on one of those outings, I went to the local supermarket with my daughter. While I was in the aisles, I spotted one of the police officers from my station. I gave a little wave but was ignored.

Weeks later, I was no better and felt so isolated. I'd had no visits from any of the other police officers to check on my welfare, not even a phone call. I guess if your injury is physical and obvious to other people, they are more accepting and supportive, but if it's a mental-health issue and can't be seen, then you are treated differently. Well, that's how I felt anyway. I was trying so hard to get better so I could return to normal and go back to work. Two weeks later, an inspector came to my house and explained that my recovery was taking too long, and that I had to move out of the police house so that someone who was working could move in. Although I was shocked by this, I wasn't surprised. I took this opportunity to return to Brisbane to be with my older children. The day we were leaving, the officer in charge came to say goodbye, but nobody else came.

When I got back to the city, I had ongoing appointments with psychologists and a psychiatrist who prescribed medication. For the next twelve months, I was in intense counselling with both of them, and spoke about many things, including the racism I had endured. Police were told to stay away from my house and not to make any contact with me, as it would hinder my recovery. They still contacted me, though; I had my former boss come to my house. He knocked on the front door, and I could see him through the glass of the door but I never answered it. He sat at the front of my house for the longest time. I ended up walking out to the front to sit in the car with him. He served me paperwork, but I can't remember what it was.

Eventually, the police service gave me the choice of either returning to work — knowing full well that I wasn't capable of this — or retiring as 'medically unfit for duties'. It was 4 November 2011. A date that has been etched into memory.

My hair had grown back after I was attacked in 2008, but my back has never healed, and I haven't healed from the psychological trauma. With an injury and trauma that prevented me from being able to perform my duties, I had to medically retire from the force. I had stayed in the police service for ten years. I would have liked to retire as a senior sergeant, but instead, I was injured while trying to arrest an ice addict.

While policing I did a lot of things I wasn't proud of. Towards the end of my time, I regretted the fact that I was in the police at all. There are some memories that play over and over. Like the time that, while doing a rotation in the traffic branch, I intercepted a vehicle that failed to stop at a stop sign. When I asked the driver their reason for doing so, he replied that he was rushing to get to the hospital, as his brother was dying. Instead of being empathetic towards the driver and letting him off with a warning, I issued him an infringement notice.

One other memory I have — and I'm ashamed to even speak of this — concerns the one sex worker I knew in my district. She was in her late twenties and addicted to heroin. I was working a shift with another female officer when I saw her standing on the corner. She was so affected by drugs that as we pulled up to the roundabout, she got in the back seat of the police vehicle and asked if we wanted her services. Instead of helping her, I issued her with a 'Notice to Appear' in court. Shortly after, she hung herself in the garage of a friend's place she was staying at. I've had to live with my actions ever since. As recruits, it's driven into you to treat people the way you would like your family member to be treated. Your mother, your father, your son or daughter. I tried my best to adhere to this, but after a while I began behaving the same as other police, just to fit in. The district that I predominantly worked in had pockets of lower socio-economic suburbs as well as wealthier suburbs. The way police treated people depended on which suburb they were from. If you lived in the wealthier suburbs and committed crime, police used their discretion and gave out warnings, in direct contrast to how they treated people from the so-called 'poorer' suburbs. This aspect of the job I found difficult, as I tried to treat everyone equally.

Towards the end of my career — and I'm talking after years — some jobs left me feeling so shit that when I got home, I would start wiping things down in my house with Pine O Cleen, and I think the smell of it made me feel better, cleansed somehow. I wiped the table, chairs, doors, door handles, light switches, my kitchen benches, and even the bloody television. I think it was the reason one of our televisions blew up once; I not only wiped the screen but the back of it as well. And if I didn't do that, I would sit on my oldest child's bed telling them about the job or shift I'd just had while they rubbed my arm — no doubt I was traumatising them. I told my therapist about this and was put on a medication that helps with depression and obsessive-compulsive disorders (OCD). I have been on this particular tablet for years now, and I only wipe down with Pine O Cleen every now and again. I believe that's how the family, especially my children, know when something is bothering me, or I am upset about something.

Policing fucked me up big time. I spent half my time in the job educating other cops about my culture, and the other half explaining the reasons I became a sworn police officer and not a police liaison officer. Not to mention the shit I put up with from other officers. You either conform to become one of them and allow yourself to be a part of the racist system and their racist ideologies about your own people, or you are in a constant battle, defending yourself. I knew a lot of cops didn't like me because I'm black, and truth be told, I didn't like them either. The friends I did make during my time — well, I don't have any contact with them anymore either.

I do have some better memories, though. Quite late in my career, I was patrolling my division with my usual partner when I saw a middle-aged female driver who appeared to be driving erratically. I was driving at the time and whacked on the sirens, indicating for her to pull off to the side of the road. I introduced myself and explained the reason for the interception. When I asked her why she was driving in that manner, she burst out crying and said that she was on her way to the nursing home where her husband lived, and that the nursing staff had just called and told her that her husband was dying. She didn't know if she would make it in time. I comforted this woman on the side of the road and told her I would make sure she got there. I told my partner to advise police communications that we needed to do a transport; he put on the police lights, and I followed behind in her car. I drove while she was seated in the passenger seat. She cried all the way,

A few weeks later, I had forgotten about this, when the counter officer at the station walked through with a bunch of flowers and card. The card was made out to me, saying: *Thank you for allowing me to be with my husband before he passed away.*

CHAPTER 26

The other day I was going through one of the boxes that contain all my photos, and the certificates of my children's achievements over the years, including their Little Athletics ribbons and time sheets. I stumbled across a black book and flicked through the pages. It was a journal I was writing when I first stopped policing in Queensland, after being diagnosed with PTSD. Looking back at what I wrote made me sad to recognise that I was at my lowest then:

> This morning I have been feeling very shit and
> negative. I went to IGA today and saw the wife of a
> police officer and she ignored me. I walked around
> the supermarket crying. The whole time I wanted to
> die. I am sick of being like this; it might be better if
> I'm not alive then I can't be like this and feel shit. I
> want to tell someone about this, but I am scared of
> their reactions. I can't help feeling like this. I'm sick
> of having anxieties over shit, negative thoughts that
> aren't real. Simple and quick.

That part of me has long gone, although, today, in certain situations, I still suffer from anxiety and panic attacks. Mostly, though, I have learnt to manage them.

When I was at the police academy and having exams every two weeks, my method of studying was to cram the night before. I would make up palm cards that I studied over and over, and then I made up mock exam questions, which my oldest child would test me on. My children were all instrumental in my time at the academy, but after becoming a cop, things changed, and my moods changed. I was very vocal about my disapproval, which did me no favours. I pretty much spent my entire time as a police officer being subjected to some form of racism, either directly or indirectly, and defending myself and my people. I don't have many regrets in my life, but my decision to become a police officer is right up there. The system is not designed for Aboriginal people. We are not meant to be police officers. In order to succeed in the police force you have to change your mentality, your views on your own people. To turn a blind eye, to not speak up about the injustices caused to your own mob, you have to effectively assimilate, *become white*, to act white and to think white. I just couldn't do that, and nor could all the other black police officers that have likewise left, both before and after I did. The treatment we have all endured has caused so much stress and trauma. I will probably have to have counselling and be on anti-depressants for the rest of my life — and it wasn't about the jobs I attended, it was about being in the job itself. I was told many times that it was good for black people to be in the police, as we could educate other police about our identity and culture. Why this heavy burden fell on my and other black cops' shoulders is beyond my comprehension. I am pretty confident that if white people were to book a holiday overseas, they would do some research about the country they were visiting, the social etiquettes, religion, or culture. Then why not do the same or offer the same courtesy for the country they reside in? Why not research the traditional owners of this country or the stolen land they occupy? The policing system is not designed for black people. It was derived from a colonial system, and it's there to cater to white people.

Recently my mother passed away from that insidious disease, cancer. She suffered for about three years, had half a lung cut out, and courses of chemotherapy and radiation to improve her chances of longevity. The treatment prolonged her life somewhat but not without considerable pain. Three years earlier, Mum had been telling me that during the night, she kept waking up struggling to breathe. Mum was a heavy smoker, but cancer was still the furthest thing from my mind. I suggested that she might have sleep apnoea and arranged an appointment for her with a specialist. Mum attended that appointment, but the specialist requested an X-ray of her lungs. The scan revealed that mum had a spot on her lower left lung, and it was cancerous.

This is really difficult to speak about — and I also don't want to speak ill of the dead — but my mother was quite racist in her later years. Especially after being with her Czech partner for thirty-odd years, who hated black people and Muslims and Turkish people and Jews. In fact, they hated anybody who wasn't white, Caucasian, what they considered the 'supreme race'. I had so many arguments with the pair of them. This and her abusive behaviour while intoxicated were the main reasons I stayed away from my mum, and also kept my children away. I didn't want my children to witness racist behaviour or violence. My job as a parent was to protect, and I certainly wasn't going to put them through what I had been through with her. I was trying my darndest to break the cycle.

When I was a kid, my mum referred to me as the 'little black bitch', which hurt me to the core. This continued into my adult life. My mum asked me on several occasions why I identified as being black when I had white blood, her blood, in me. She asked me why I chose to have my children to black men when white men are better. I'm not sure if my other siblings were exposed to this or not, but they knew mum and her partner had their racist ideologies, and it was like a running joke to them. It wasn't a joke to me, though, and I believe I was the only one that spoke up. I would pull them up on their racist comments and got into a lot of verbal stoushes with them. One day I asked my mum why she was so racist towards practising Muslims when she hadn't even spoken to one or met one. I was actually crying when I asked her this. I was so hurt and frustrated. And when Mum was in palliative care, her treating doctor was — yep, you guessed it — an Arab, and he was the best, so caring and compassionate.

When my mother's father passed away in a nursing home in Victoria, I was stuck working in the floods in Queensland. I had been sent to a small town, along with other police. The town was being ravaged by rising water levels due to torrential rains, and its low-lying areas were going under. Our role was to assist with the evacuation of residents and to prevent looting, which was already occurring. The river level rose at a fast pace, the highest it had been in decades, and the rapids were fast flowing, with cows and large trees being swept away in the river. So I never went to my grandfather's funeral. I couldn't afford the airfares to get down there in time; I also hate funerals. I believe that they are for the living not the dead — so much so, that when I go, I'm not having a funeral. I just want to be laid to rest, and that's that. I don't even want a coffin — I want cardboard or a shroud, something environmentally friendly, and I definitely don't want a church service.

Now, fast forward a couple of years to when my dad's father passed away. While plans were being made for his funeral, I got a phone call from my mother asking if I was intending on going to his funeral, and I said yes. Well, the shit hit the fan. She asked, 'Why are you going to your black grandfather's funeral when you couldn't go to your white grandfather's funeral?' I was so upset by this question. She knew how close I was to my grandfather — or, as she put it, my *black* grandfather.

Months later, my mum and her partner were visiting Brisbane, where I and most of my siblings lived. They never came and saw me but stayed with my brothers and little sister. I didn't even know they were there. I found out in passing, weeks after, during a conversation with my dad. I cried on the phone to him when I found out. I asked my dad, 'Why doesn't Mum love me like she does the other kids?'

One night, late, while I was watching television, I received a text message. I knew it was important because I don't usually get texts or phone calls late at night. It was a text from my mum, telling me that she was in hospital. She asked if I could come up to where she was, eight hours away in Sydney. I texted back, telling her that I would be there tomorrow. I lived in the countryside and had to travel a few hours to the airport to reach my flight. I telephoned my youngest daughter and asked if she would come with me. That night, I booked our flights, and got us seats right at the front of the aeroplane so that when it landed, we could be the first off. I packed a bag of clothes, not really knowing how long I was going to be away for.

The flight, although only one hour, seemed to take forever. I was thinking about my mum for the whole flight, thinking about what condition she was in. Despite our differences, my mum and I spoke on the telephone every day for hours and hours, but towards the end, she was finding it difficult to talk, so she texted instead. Mum would send me the longest texts. One time, I was driving with my family, so her message went through the car speaker. Siri went on and on reading it out, and it sounded so funny. She would give me updates of her illness, and I would comfort her with positive affirmations. On several occasions, I tried to convince her that she needed to call an ambulance and go to hospital, but she never went, saying that she was okay. I truly believe that Mum was frightened to go to hospital because she knew that if she went, she may not have come out.

I was deep in thought when the plane jolted as it landed on the tarmac. I unbuckled my seat belt and stood up, grabbed my overhead luggage, and exited the plane. We ran as fast as we could through the airport to the taxi stand, where we got the first available cab, and I gave instructions to take us to the hospital. The drive took about 30 minutes. I could have taken the train — which was a lot less expensive — but I wanted to get there quickly.

Walking along the sterile corridor of the hospital, I could feel my heartbeat with every step. I finally made it to the room and noticed there were three other patients. I rushed up to my mum as she lay on the bed, giving her a big kiss and a long cuddle. Mum was wearing a pair of pyjamas, and she had a fluffy grey dressing gown on top of the white hospital blanket covering her legs. Mum affectionately named this dressing gown 'Bugsy', saying that when she wore it, she looked like a big rabbit. I wanted to just hold onto my mum and never let her go. I asked for an update and the medical staff told me that while I was travelling, a series of tests had been conducted: blood tests and scans. I knew it was bad, but I tried to stay optimistic.

My mum and I had a lot of disagreements over the years, but as I looked into her eyes on this day, all that was forgotten. Mum was hooked up to a ventilator for her breathing, and her pulse and blood pressure were taken regularly. Several hours later, a doctor came in to conduct his rounds. He approached Mum's bedside and told her that her cancer had spread to her heart, and she had very little time left to live. My heart almost stopped. I studied Mum's face as she heard this news; she was so brave and strong. I'm not sure that if I was told that news, I could be as brave as her. I grabbed my daughter's hand and squeezed it tight. I felt my eyes welling up with tears; my eyes were stinging, but I didn't want to upset my mum with my reaction to this news. I wanted to be strong. While nurses were tending to my mum, I took this moment to get out of the room. My daughter and I sobbed. I gained my composure and called my siblings — who were all interstate — to tell them the devastating news. I went back in the room beside Mum, and I hugged her tight and we both cried.

A few days later, my brothers and sisters arrived, as palliative care was arranged for my mum in another hospital, some suburbs away. Mum and Bugsy were transported in an ambulance to the palliative care hospice. The smell of death lingered in the corridor of this hospice. It was a smell I was accustomed to. My brothers and sisters stayed for a week, but then had to return to their homes. I stayed with Mum, even after my daughter had to go home as well. I stayed for six weeks. During this time, I asked

Mum all the hard questions. Where she wanted to be buried, what she wanted to wear, what music she wanted. Mum planned her funeral with me.

It was while I was sitting with Mum that I remembered a job I had been to years earlier, a job where a middle-aged woman was found deceased on her bed, wearing nothing but a pair of bikini briefs. We notified her next of kin — her three adult children. When I saw them arrive, I went outside to greet them and offered my condolences. I said, 'I'm so sorry for your loss.' They said, 'We're not. We hated her — she was nothing but a violent drunk.' This was followed by an awkward silence. It reminded me of the relationship I had with my mother, and was something I would have said prior to spending the last six weeks of her life with her.

There was a moment, when I was sitting beside Mum, that I had the sense that I finally understood her. The reasons why she was so angry and bitter towards Dad. She was not only angry, she was also hurt and grieving. Grieving the loss of her marriage to the father of her children. It became clear to me that when Dad left, her life had forever changed.

Mum was moved into her own room. I knew it was getting close to her end, and I was giving my siblings updates all the time. My younger brother decided that he needed to be there, so he drove 16 hours. I was so relieved that someone else was with me. I was struggling, both physically and emotionally. I was only sleeping three hours in each 24-hour period. I slept on the floor beside my mum until staff gave me a recliner chair. I never left the room unless needed. My mum couldn't speak by then, so I had to speak for her. When Mum looked at me, I knew what she wanted. I knew when she was in pain, so I would call for the nurse to give her pain relief. I knew when she needed oxygen to help her breathe. I called the nurse to give Mum the oxygen. I knew when she took her last breath. I thought I was strong until Mum died. Her death was harder than every other death I had encountered. I was present when my grandfather and grandmother died, but this hit me harder. I just hope that Mum knew I had forgiven her a long time ago for walking out on us kids.

Although I was a police officer, it has not defined who I am. I still have the same attributes, integrity, ethics, and morals I've always had — I just don't wear a uniform. I have since moved on to other projects that bring me joy and happiness, such as family research and learning my traditional language.

I spent my police career as the single mother of three beautiful children. They have now turned into three beautiful adults. I am now the kukun of twins, Nanwan and Yeerung, and hopefully more to come. I have also been in a relationship with the love of my life for some years now. It wasn't easy at the beginning, due to my distrust and insecurities, but I got through it with his help. I have learnt to love again and to be loved. I know that my grandmother would be extremely proud of me for telling my story, but especially proud for telling hers, and if I could, I would say *thank you* to both my grandparents: for teaching me language, culture through song and dance, and all their stories.

I was never told that I was Aboriginal. I just always knew. It is not something that is discussed — they don't sit you down and tell you. It was just the way it was. Writing this book has been somewhat healing for me. I am still an angry little black woman, though, due to the atrocities that my ancestors have endured since invasion, and through ongoing colonisation. I'm angry about the way police continue to treat my people; I'm angry about the over-representation of my people among this country's incarcerated population. I'm angry about the deaths in custody of my people, and I am furious that to date, no police have ever been held accountable. After spending time in the police force, and witnessing all that I have, I know that I have been complicit. I feel terrible about this. I now believe in abolitionism — not only of the police, but also of prisons and youth detention centres, especially for my people, Aboriginal and Torres Strait Islanders. Many crimes committed by my people are drug- or alcohol-related. I don't believe these are criminal matters; they are health problems. Us mob have Cultural Law/Lore that has been practised since long before colonisation, and we continue to utilise it. I don't have all the answers. I just know the current system isn't working.

Writing this has been difficult. I know that my story isn't unique or rare, but what sets my story apart from others is that I have written about it. If I inspire just one person to write a book or even put pen to paper, I'll be happy.

Because everyone has a story — we just need to listen to them long enough.

ACKNOWLEDGEMENTS

I would like to acknowledge the traditional owners, past and present, all over and wherever you may be reading this book from. I would also like to acknowledge my elders past and present, the first peoples of the Gunai/Kurnai nation. My ancestors who long before me survived massacres and genocide. A special acknowledgement goes to my grandparents Linda and Carl Turner, and my father, John Gorrie PSM, who has been my constant, and been there for me through all my ups and downs. You have been my pillar of strength, my motivator, and the deadliest father. I know that when I was a cop you were so proud of me, but it got hard, Dad.

To all the strong black women in my life, I thank you. My grandmother, the late Linda Edith Turner (nee Gorrie), the staunchest and the strongest of them all. A special thanks to my Aunty Dot Moffatt, my cousin and best friend, Sharon Berry, and my best friend and tidda, Deanne Johnson. You get me through most days, and I am truly grateful. Thank you also to Melissa Lucashenko, Dr Chelsea Watego, and Nakkiah Lui.

A special gratitude goes to my lifelong best friends Ninette and Tanya. Tanya, you and your family became a special extended family to my children and me. You were the one who encouraged me to get my eyebrows waxed for the first time, so for that, my eyebrows and I thank you. I truly thank you for all the times when I had no food, and you were the one who fed us. You were always the person I went to when I had bad days, and I love you heaps for that.

Ninette, you are my best friend from our high school days, and although I take off this way and that way, we always find each other. When we do, it's as if no time has passed, and that's what I love about you most. Throughout my teens, you and your family took me in, and if I wasn't at yours, you were at mine.

I would like to dedicate this book to my three brilliant, amazing, and beautiful children, Nayuka, Paul, and Likarri. Without you three, I am nothing. Everything I have done has been for you. You have given me the strength to speak up and speak out. I am so grateful for you all, and I am so proud of all your achievements and successes.

I am grateful and inspired by all the hard work you all do through your fierce, relentless, unwavering, tenacious, and tireless activism and advocacy. You support: the fight against family violence and violence against women and children; abolishing police and prisons; abolishing youth detention centres; climate justice; safe spaces for Aboriginal and Torres Strait Islander mob, as well as the LGTBQI+ family/community; improving the wellbeing of our people; fighting for land rights; fighting against racism against our mob and other minority groups; decriminalising and abolishing the barbaric legislations that wrongfully incarcerate our mob; and the fight against black deaths in custody.

I am deeply remorseful for all the poor choices I have made in my life that have affected you. I know that as a result of my poor choices, I have inherently caused you all anxiety. For that, I am deeply sorry. I love you guys immensely; you are and will continue to be my best friends.

I would also like to acknowledge my little brother and to tell him that although I have spoken about some alcohol-fuelled events that have occurred, I know that's all they were — because without alcohol, you are the best brother and an amazing person, and I love you heaps. You have always been there for my children and me, and you have saved my life so many times, and most times without even knowing it.

I would like to thank my husband, Ryan, and although we aren't married the white way, we are the black way (married up). You have been on this journey with me the whole way through, supporting and encouraging me with copious amounts of tea and coffee while I typed away and cried during this process. It has been an eventful journey, but I wouldn't change a thing.

I have a special gratitude for MB and KS, who were always there for me in the job, and who listened when I was subjected to racism and bullying. MB — you were there during my formative years, right from the start, and although we have lost contact due to different paths, you will always be my little brother. KS — you and I had each other's backs for years, and with you by my side, I had the most memorable moments. You were my best mate in the job. It was your humour and your friendship that got me through most shifts, and although we have lost contact, you will always be my brother.

I would like to acknowledge all staff at Scribe, and, in particular, Marika Webb-Pullman, who believed in my story and has supported me throughout the process, and my publicist, Cora Roberts.

VKR OSCAR 700 14364 GOLF SHOW ME OFF.

GLOSSARY

boondie — club/stick

bunty — arsehole/anus

Country — traditional lands

djillawah — urinate/toilet

deadly — good

dooligah —big foot/hairy man

gammin — only joking

gubba — white people

gungai — police

humpy — a shelter built by Aboriginal people to live in

kukun — mother's mother (grandmother)

mob — my people, Aboriginal people

moonas — head lice

mrarji — ghosts/spirits

tidda — sister

yarn — story/talk

yarndi — marijuana